getting into

Oxford &
Cambridge

2010 Entry

Oxford & Cambridge

2010 Entry

Sarah Alakija

12th Edition

Getting into Oxford & Cambridge: 2010 Entry

This 12th edition published in 2009 by Trotman Publishing, an imprint of Crimson Publishing Limited, Westminster House, Kew Road, Richmond, Surrey TW9 2ND.

© Trotman Publishing 2008, 2009

© Trotman 1987, 1989, 1991, 1994, 1996, 1999, 2001, 2003, 2005, 2007
Reprinted 2005, 2006, 2007, 2008.

Author Sarah Alakija
11th edition by Natalie Lancer
Editions 7–10, 12 Sarah Alakija

British Library Cataloguing in Publication Data
A catalogue record for this book is available from the British Library

ISBN 978-1-84455-193-4

Typeset by IDSUK (DataConnection) Ltd

Printed and bound in the UK by the MPG Books Group

Contents

About the author

Sarah Alakija studied at the University of Cambridge, reading Spanish and Portuguese for Part I of her Tripos and law for Part II. She is currently Vice Principal at MPW London and will shortly take up the post of Principal of an independent west London college.

Acknowledgements

The author would like to thank all of her students who helped with this and all the previous editions of the book. Their input is invaluable in making this book so helpful and realistic to potential applicants. She would also like to thank the following people for all their help, advice and patience: Jamie Charters; Mario Di Clemente; Matthew Judd and Petrouchka Stafford.

Introduction

This book intends to give you a flavour of what the application process for getting into Oxford and Cambridge is like. It is a process revered the world over for its ability to select some of the finest minds in the world and to welcome them to the institutions renowned for the discovery of some of the most life-changing things that you or I can think of. From Isaac Newton to Stephen Hawking, some of the finest minds have been educated here, and do you know what? You could be too!

The aim of this book is not to reproduce information that is readily available, and indeed you should read, on the Oxford and Cambridge admissions websites, but to explain how to access and how to use this information and, most importantly, how to make sense of it.

It is sad, but true, that even if you put yourself in the best possible position to get a place, you may still be unsuccessful. But, take heart, there are many excellent universities and if you really are committed, you will have an interesting and fulfilling life whatever you do. However, let's get on with maximising your chances of entry into Oxford and Cambridge. As with many things, it is best to plan ahead. Ideally you should be reading this in your first year of sixth form. This is because, unlike applications to other universities, which can be sent until the January of your A2 year without penalty (you can apply after January but universities are not under obligation to give your application the same consideration as for applications submitted before January), the deadline for application for Oxford and Cambridge is 15 October of your A2 year – extremely early in the first term. In other words, the bulk of the preparation has to be done in the previous term and throughout the summer.

The first thing you should do is to order the undergraduate prospectus for both universities. Although all the information is available online, you may find it easier to see the information in paper form. To order the Oxford prospectus, ring the Oxford Colleges Admissions Office on 01865 288000, or email undergraduate.admissions@admin.ox.ac.uk, or you can order it online at www.ox.ac.uk/admissions/prospectuses.html. For Cambridge, call the Cambridge Admissions Office on 01223 333308, or email admissions@cam.ac.uk or you can order it online at www.cam.ac.uk/admissions/undergraduate/publications/prospectus.html.

In addition, the student unions at both universities produce an 'alternative prospectus', which will give you another perspective on life at the university. See www.ousu.org/prospective-students/ap and www.cusu.cam.ac.uk/prospective/prospectus.

01 Choosing a university, choosing a college

Should I apply to Oxbridge?

It is often said that Oxbridge is a 'self-selection' process. This means that the people who consider going are the people who should be considering it. Your teacher may have suggested it to you, or you know someone who went there or perhaps you have read about it or seen a film where they feature. Whatever the situation, you have realised that there is something special about the universities and you are wondering if one of them is for you. The short answer is: they probably are. Why? Because there are so many different colleges that make up Oxford and Cambridge, from traditional to avant-garde, historic to modern, left wing to right wing, that there is bound to be one that suits you.

It is important to understand that students at Oxford or Cambridge work extremely hard. Typically you will write at least one essay of about 2,500 words a week for a tutorial (Oxford) or a supervision (Cambridge). Although it will vary between subjects, in your first year you will have lectures to attend (for sciences about three hours a day and for arts about five hours a week) and perhaps a small technical class to attend. For some subjects lectures are optional. In the second and third years you have more choice over what to attend. You will be given book and journal lists and you will spend a lot of time undertaking independent study. There are also exams (called Collections at Oxford) at the beginning of every term at Oxford and at the end of each year at Cambridge.

Oxford and Cambridge welcome students from all ethnic and financial backgrounds, those with disabilities, with children and also mature students. The next section is concerned with the practicalities of this.

What are Oxford and Cambridge like?

Memorable. Unforgettable. Drop into your local library and you'll find a selection of books containing reminiscences of Oxford or

Cambridge, not to mention the inevitable crop of guide books to the cities. Turn to the fiction section and you will discover that many novelists have used these cities and their universities as settings for their work. Waugh's *Brideshead Revisited*, C. P. Snow's *The Masters* and Max Beerbohm's *Zuleika Dobson* are some of the most well known. More recently the dramatisation of Sharpe's *Porterhouse Blue* and the Inspector Morse series have brought Cambridge and Oxford, respectively, to the television.

Few graduates of Oxford or Cambridge will deny that their university experience has in many ways affected their whole life, and most will need little prompting to express vivid memories of those three or four important years. These educational institutions arouse passions and affection. Everybody seems to have his or her own ideas about what these institutions are like.

By any standards Oxford and Cambridge are large universities. Cambridge has a student body of about 15,000 of which some 10,500 are undergraduates, and Oxford has a student body of about 16,500 of which some 11,500 are undergraduates. Both are ancient religious foundations: the first Oxford college was established in 1249, some 35 years before the first college at Cambridge. Both are famed for their research and teaching, and both offer a wide range of courses. If they sound rather similar institutions, it is not surprising . . . they are. Few at either Oxford or Cambridge may agree though, as pride in each university's own character is strong. Competition between them lies deeper than the Boat Race, but the rivalry is friendly and continues as a tradition.

Nevertheless, we talk about Oxford and Cambridge in the same breath. It has even been necessary to invent a collective word to describe them. 'Oxbridge' has been accepted into the language and can be found in most English dictionaries. We see the two universities in the same light and in the same league. What binds them together in everybody's minds, in a unique alliance, is a combination of history and standards. Both reach levels of excellence that are respected throughout the world and thus they attract teaching staff of a very high calibre. That is not to say that there aren't other good, indeed great, universities in Britain. There are, and they should be considered seriously in your application.

Each of the two universities is made up of many colleges. The course content of the subject is set centrally at the university level. The university is the equivalent of the exam boards and it holds lectures in large lecture halls for you to attend and practicals where applicable. Sometimes these are optional and sometimes they are compulsory – it depends on the subject.

The colleges are a bit like boarding school. You live and eat there and you also get taught by your tutors there in tutorials/supervisions or in classes. If your college does not have a specialist in a particular part of the course then you may go to another college for that part, or in a small faculty you will be taught in that faculty. The faculties and colleges occupy different sites at the universities and you will have to walk or cycle between them.

Is it just standards that set Oxford and Cambridge apart?

Some people believe that Oxford and Cambridge's exclusivity stems from the way they operate and the way they have developed their collegiate and tutorial system. It's a system that other universities have tried to emulate but not entirely successfully. It is a unique model that lies at the very centre of the character of Oxbridge.

To an outsider, the system must seem a little bizarre. No modern planner would devise a university in this way. In fact, the system may appear untidy and even wasteful of prodigious teaching talent. However, it works well, and for the undergraduates who make their way to Oxford or Cambridge it provides an excellent teaching base.

Teaching takes place at the universities in a different way from others. Although you are a member of a college, you are unlikely to have many of your classes there. Lectures are delivered on a faculty basis and so will take place away from your college. If one of the papers you are studying is taught by a tutor at your college, then you will have your supervisions (as they are known in Cambridge) or tutorials (as they are known in Oxford) there at the college. These will take the form of a small discursive class which is a forum for giving and receiving criticism on work that you have undertaken. Other papers that you may be reading as part of your degree may well be taught at another college where the specialist tutor resides. This means that you will have classes all over the town!

Bear in mind when you are considering whether to apply that the terms are very short at both of these universities. Although at first this may seem like a good idea in that you will have good long holidays, stop and think for a moment. What it actually means is that you will be fitting an awful lot of work into a couple of months at a time. And remember, you will be worked hard. These are not two of the finest universities in the world without somebody doing a lot of work. I will never forget calling a friend who was at a university in the north of England. At the time, I had just finished my first term at Cambridge. I asked her if she was working hard. She laughed and told me that she had just been set her first history essay! This was after I had done eight weeks' worth of work. And I can assure you that I had done at least two pieces of work per week during that time! Don't let it put you off though. If you love your subject, you will make and enjoy this commitment.

Can I afford to go to Oxbridge?

Most universities, including Oxford and Cambridge, charge home students £3,145 (correct for 2009 entry) for annual tuition fees, which increases in line with inflation. You can get a student loan to cover the cost of the fees, which you do not have to repay until after you have graduated and are earning a salary of £15,000 or more. There are also living costs that cannot be deferred. This includes rent, clothes and food. Both universities provide college accommodation (although the length of time they provide it varies considerably between colleges), which is substantially cheaper than commercial rates, and you only have to pay it when you are 'in residence' and not in your holidays. A typical rent is between £65 and £80 per week for a room for 30 weeks and for an en suite room it is between £80 and £100 per week. Meals in the colleges are heavily subsidised and are usually of excellent quality. In fact, Merton College in Oxford was endowed with a sum of money by one of its alumni to ensure the food is of top quality.

Both Oxford and Cambridge are very keen to make it clear that if you need financial assistance, they will give it to you. At the back of the Oxford prospectus, it says:

> If you can get in, we can help out . . . At Oxford your mind is the only asset we're interested in.
>
> **Oxford Prospectus, 2008**

The Cambridge website describes the Cambridge Bursary Scheme:

> We are committed to the principle that no UK student should be deterred from applying to the University of Cambridge because of financial concerns, and that no student should have to leave because of financial difficulties. As a result we have one of the most extensive financial support programmes in the UK to ensure that students can meet the cost of the Cambridge education, regardless of background.

Bursaries at both universities are worth approximately £12,000–£13,000 over four years. In addition, most of the colleges have large endowments and can therefore provide their own bursaries, grants and scholarships. They also give prizes in the form of financial rewards for academic excellence in tutorials/supervisions and exams. Telephone the colleges individually to find out what is on offer.

If you are lucky enough to be a near-professional singer or organist and would like to spend at least six hours a week singing in the college chapel or playing the organ, you can also apply for a music or choral award. The application deadline for this is a month earlier than for regular undergraduate UCAS applications (see Appendix 2, Key dates). Visit www.admissions.ox.ac.uk/orgscholars and http://131.111.8.46/admissions/undergraduate/musicawards/index.html for more information.

Some colleges interview music or choral scholars in September and others in December. There are also different requirements for music or choral scholars at different colleges. For example, you may have to be trained in the Anglican tradition or may have to be the right kind of baritone.

Mature students

A mature student is defined as someone who is 21 years old by 1 October of the year in which they start their course. If you are a mature student, you may prefer one of the colleges that admits a good number of mature students or exclusively admits mature students (see Appendix 3).

Mature students are very much welcomed at both Oxford and Cambridge, and both universities have dedicated mature colleges (Oxford has one and Cambridge has four). The admissions process is the same as for non-mature students and the academic standard required is equally high for both. Naturally, work and life experience are taken into account as well as previous academic qualifications. You are advised to contact a college directly before making your application in order to discuss your suitability.

Young students

There is no minimum age for applicants, but the university will want you to demonstrate that you have the maturity to study in a university environment. If you will be younger than 18 in the year of entry it may be best to take a year out and improve your life skills.

Students who want to take a gap year

Taking a gap year for something concrete and worthwhile may not be an issue. If you are applying for languages and you haven't studied one of the languages before, the admissions tutors might even encourage you to take a gap year. Conversely, if you are applying for maths, the admissions tutor may feel that you may forget your maths and may need some reassuring that what you are doing in your gap year will augment your studies and not help you forget them. Policies about gap years vary between individual colleges and subjects and so if you know you want to have a gap year, consult the admissions tutor well in advance. That said, if they think you are good, they won't mind if you take a gap year, if you can demonstrate how it will be useful and productive.

About one in five students coming to Cambridge takes a gap year before starting their studies. This year out proves a very useful time in which to improve skills, earn money, travel and generally gain maturity and self-reliance.

Cambridge Prospectus, 2007/8

Disabled students

Disabled students are welcomed at both universities. There may be some practical considerations such as making sure you choose a college that is near your faculty so that you will not have to walk far. The admissions offices at both universities can help you with this so be sure to telephone them as early as possible. Of course, there are a whole range of disabilities, which include dyslexia and visual or hearing impairments. Your disability must be declared on the UCAS form. Remember that people who declare a disability are in no way at a disadvantage. The key is to contact the admissions office as early as possible.

Student parents

Both Oxford and Cambridge welcome applications from prospective students who have children. Several colleges provide accommodation for couples and families. Ring the admissions office for more information. Also, some colleges have their own nurseries (see Appendix 3). There are also some university-wide nurseries.

Students from ethnic minorities

Cambridge is taking active steps to particularly welcome students from ethnic minorities and has set up the Group to Encourage Ethnic Minority Applications (GEEMA). Email geema@cao.cam.ac.uk and the Oxford Admissions Office for more information.

International students

International students too are welcomed at both Oxford and Cambridge. International students make up less than 10% of undergraduates at Cambridge and 14% of undergraduates at Oxford. However, the percentages of overseas students are much higher for postgraduate study: at Cambridge 50% of postgraduates and at Oxford 63% of postgraduates are international students. In order to study at Oxford and Cambridge, your English must be of a high standard. This is measured by your performance in the IELTS (International English Language Testing System) exam: you need a score of at least 7.0 in each section (speaking, listening, writing and reading) or a GCSE in English Language at grade C or above. See the university prospectus for more details.

The costs of studying at a UK university for an international student are much higher than for a home student. The tuition fees range from £9,327 to £12,219 for most courses although clinical medicine costs in excess of £20,000. See http://131.111.8.46/admissions/undergraduate/international/costs.htm and www.admissions.ox.ac.uk/finance/costs/#uni for more details about costs, and www.ielts.org for more information about the IELTS exam and where it can be sat. Information on how to apply is given later in the book (see Chapter 6).

Gay, lesbian, bisexual and transsexual (GLBT) students

Oxford and Cambridge are totally pluralist universities. Not only is there a central GLBT society but each college also has its own GLBT society. There are plenty of events to help you feel totally comfortable.

Should I apply to Oxford or Cambridge?

You can apply to Oxford or Cambridge but not both. They are both equally prestigious and both have wonderful facilities such as a plethora of world-class libraries and world-class teaching. So how do you decide which one to apply to?

Choosing a university by subject offered

There are various subjects that Oxford offers and which Cambridge does not and vice versa.

Subjects you can study at Cambridge but not at Oxford:

- architecture
- economics (as a stand-alone subject; in Oxford you do a combined course of economics and management)
- education studies
- land economy
- languages: Dutch, Anglo-Saxon, Norse and Celtic
- management studies (as a stand-alone subject; in Oxford you do a combined course of economics and management)
- natural sciences (although at Oxford all the sciences are offered but not in the same combination)
- philosophy (as a stand-alone subject; in Oxford you do a combined course of philosophy, politics and economics)
- social and political science (SPS)
- veterinary medicine.

Subjects you can study at Oxford but not at Cambridge:

- languages: Sanskrit, Czech with Slovak
- philosophy, politics and economics (PPE)
- psychology, philosophy and physiology (PPP)
- separate sciences: although you do have to do modules in other science subjects as well.

Subjects you can study at both universities:

- archaeology and anthropology
- classics
- computer science
- engineering
- English
- geography
- history
- human sciences
- law
- modern and medieval languages
- music
- Oriental studies (at Oxford) and Asian and Middle Eastern studies course (at Cambridge)
- theology and religious studies.

To see which courses are offered at Oxford and Cambridge go to: www.admissions.ox.ac.uk and www.cam.ac.uk/admissions/undergraduate, respectively. If both universities offer the same course, how do you decide which one to apply for? First, you should understand that just because the title is the same, it does not mean the course is the same. For example, economics can be studied at both Oxford and

Cambridge, but at Oxford it is either within the PPE or economics and management course. The economics modules in economics and management are influenced by management, so if you take a finance module it would be mathematically based but within management. There is great flexibility as to which modules you can take. At Cambridge, economics is the main course. The founder of macroeconomics (Keynes) went to Cambridge and the course is more traditional. Economics at Cambridge has more compulsory mathematical elements than that at Oxford, although one can opt to do mathematical options at Oxford.

It is important to read the course details carefully, which can be found in the prospectus or in the online prospectus, so that you can make an informed decision as to which course would be more suitable for you. Here are some of the issues which you may find arising.

Cambridge

It is often said that one of the great attractions of Cambridge is the flexibility of its Tripos system. The name Tripos is said to be derived from the three-legged stool that undergraduates in medieval times would sit on for their oral examinations.

Each course, or Tripos, is usually divided into two parts, Part I and Part II. It's quite easy to understand how Part I works. It's taken after either one year (e.g. economics) or two years (e.g. English). Often, a two-year Part I is divided into IA and IB with examinations at the end of *each* of the first two years (e.g. geography). The real flexibility kicks in following the successful completion of Part I. One obvious option is to specialise further by completing Part II in the same Tripos. For three-year courses, if Part I takes two years, Part II takes one year and vice versa. However, many students switch Tripos after Part I, sometimes involving a one-year Part II, sometimes a two-year Part II.

Switching of Tripos is one way of ending up with a four-year undergraduate course. In addition, natural science and mathematics students have the option of adding a Part III, while engineering students take Parts IA, IB, IIA and IIB over four years, leading ultimately to the award of MEng.

Oxford

As in Cambridge, students in Oxford have to pass exams in two parts. However, one major difference at Oxford is that you won't have to take examinations at the end of each year, as is the case in many Cambridge Tripos. The Preliminary Examinations (or 'Prelims') are taken at the end of the first year (except for experimental psychology and PPP, where they are taken at the end of the second term), and the Final Examinations ('Finals') are taken at the end of the third year. Just to confuse matters, the first set of exams is sometimes called Honour Moderations (or 'Mods'), examples being: mathematics courses, archaeology and anthropology, classics, history and geography. Classics Mods are taken at the end of five terms.

In general there are rather more courses at Oxford which are designed to take (rather than having the option of taking) four years. The joint honours courses of mathematics and philosophy and physics and philosophy, as well as classics, take four years. Mathematics itself, physics and earth sciences can take either three or four years (your choice), but in the case of molecular and cellular biochemistry, chemistry, engineering and metallurgy, students would normally be expected to progress to the fourth, research-based, year leading to the award of the master's degree.

On balance, the two universities have converged rather than diverged in recent years and you should not overstate the differences at interview. Where Cambridge has the flexibility of its Tripos system, Oxford has more in the way of joint honours courses. For years, archaeology and anthropology was offered only at Cambridge. Now it is offered at Oxford too. Keep the differences that remain clearly in focus:

- lots of courses in Cambridge with exams each year
- individual differences between three- and four-year options at the two universities
- no real equivalent to SPS available at Oxford
- no real equivalent to PPE available at Cambridge
- less ability to specialise in a single science subject at Cambridge
- no facility for studying economics or philosophy as a single subject at Oxford
- no facility for studying psychology as a single subject at Cambridge.

Research the similarities and differences as they apply to your particular subject choice and don't forget what you have discovered when it comes to interview. The next step is to go on an open day or to walk round the universities and colleges, and this is discussed below.

Open days

Both universities run open days throughout the year but mainly between April and July of your AS year. You can find out when they are at www.admissions.ox.ac.uk/opendays/open1.html and www.cam.ac.uk/admissions/undergraduate/opendays. The next step is to ring up the college or faculty and book yourself a place.

Although the faculties also conduct open days, it is much more informative to sign up for a college open day. It does not matter which college you choose, as you will get to visit your chosen faculty as well as seeing the college.

What are you meant to be looking for at an open day?

First you are going to get an overall impression of the place. Walk to the library and to the faculty buildings (use the map at the back of this book). How far away are they from your proposed college? Would you prefer to be at a college that is on the river or that is near the library? Do you want to be at a sporty college? Ask any students whom you encounter how they like their college.

The open day is also an opportunity to meet the tutors and ask them some questions. You can make quite an impression on them at this point, so make sure you are smartly dressed and you ask sensible questions. You may want to know about aspects of the course. You could ask them to recommend a book for you to read. Talk to a student who is on your course and ask them what it is like. There will normally be a talk from the dean (like a headmaster) of the college and a tour of the faculty. You will almost certainly be given lunch for free.

Ultimately, you have to be able to see yourself at your chosen college. After the formal proceedings of the open day have concluded visit other colleges and write down your impressions. Once you have a short list you can fill in other aspects of the college using the prospectus, such as for how many years it offers accommodation in college.

Your school may also organise trips to Oxford or Cambridge, for which you should sign up. If you miss the open days and your school does not do trips to both universities then just go up for the day and look around yourself. The maps at the back of this book should help you. When you visit the colleges on non-open days, make sure you tell the college porters that you are a prospective student and that your parent/friend is accompanying you as otherwise you may be asked to pay a tourist entrance fee, which you do not need to pay. Be insistent on this point even if the porter still wants to charge you – ask to see the head porter if necessary. Tourists pay at least £3 per person per college, which can work out to be rather expensive considering there are about 40 colleges. Some colleges are for graduates only so it is necessary to do some research and plan your route before you go. Many colleges are clustered together but some are further away.

Choosing a college

Criteria for choosing a college

Oxford has 30 colleges and six permanent private halls (discussed below) and Cambridge has 29 colleges. So how do you choose a college to which to apply?

Read through the description of each college. Not all colleges offer all subjects and you should find out what subjects are not offered in the general prospectus. Oxford produces a handy table that summarises this information at www.admissions.ox.ac.uk/colleges/availab.pdf. For Cambridge you will have to click on each college separately (it may be easier to read the hard copy of the prospectus).

In addition there are two more prospectuses you can consult. When you have narrowed your choices down a little, contact each college individually and ask for a copy of its prospectus. This will give you more of a flavour of the college. It will tell you what clubs, societies, sports facilities and traditions it has (although remember that most clubs and societies are run centrally and there are hundreds to sign up to!). Each Junior Common Room (JCR) also produces a student-written 'alternative prospectus'; this is less formal and gives you an idea of the student perspective of the college. Again contact the college or ask for the email of the JCR president to order a copy. All prospectuses will be sent to you free of charge.

There are various factors that you may like to consider when choosing a college.

- Would you prefer to spend three or four years in a small college where you will get to know everyone in all years (about 40 people in each year) or would you prefer to be in a large college (about 120 people in each year)?
- Would you like to live near the city centre (remember that Oxford and Cambridge are both very small anyway) or further away? Colleges that are further away tend to have a very close-knit atmosphere as people socialise in college a lot more. If you like sleeping in, would you like your college to be near your faculty so you can roll out of bed to attend lectures? You might like to find out the gender balance. When you visit the college, ask a student what the male–female ratio is. It used to be that, until relatively recently, all colleges were single sex. Some

colleges still have this legacy, in that some former male colleges have a greater ratio of men to women.

- Does the library have long opening hours?
- Do you want to be in a college with old or modern buildings?

It is important to find out if the college offers accommodation for the duration of your studies or whether you will have to find a house to share after the first year. Some people like living in a house with their friends but there are associated problems: landlords that do not sort out broken central heating quickly, houses that are far away from your college. Also remember that often, colleges can accommodate you in student flats that you can share with your friends, and the college will look after you much better than a landlord. Most college accommodation is in single rooms, perhaps with an en suite bathroom, but more usually shared bathrooms on one staircase.

You may like to take a less emotional approach to choosing a college and look at the league tables that rank colleges according to how well the undergraduates did in their final exams. These are published by various newspapers, including *The Sunday Times* university guide. Note though, that they are not particularly endorsed by the universities themselves. (In Oxford the league table is called the Norrington Table (Table 1) and in Cambridge it is called the Tompkins Table (Table 2).) Degrees obtained at the college are scored in the following way: five points for a first; three for a 2:1; two for a 2:2 and one for a third. The score shown in Tables 1 and 2 is the percentage of total points available.

Permanent private halls

Students admitted to permanent private halls (Table 3) are full members of the university and for all intents and purposes these halls are the same as colleges. They are mostly very old and have a different history from the colleges. Subjects offered tend to be philosophy and theology, and at some of the permanent private halls many of the students are planning to be ordained as priests. Some halls do have entry restrictions but most will accept applications from people of any cultural background. I have included some brief notes about them for completeness in Appendix 3.

How important are the statistics?

Students often spend hours poring over the prospectuses and statistics trying to work out which college is easiest to get an offer from for

Table 1: Norrington table – University of Oxford. College undergraduate degree classifications 2007/08 (sorted by rank)

College	Score	Rank
Merton	77.17	1
St John's	75.96	2
Balliol	75.00	3
Magdalen	74.11	4
Christ Church	72.99	5
New	71.54	6
Queen's	71.11	7
Jesus	70.64	8
Lincoln	70.50	9
St Hugh's	70.00	10
Corpus Christi	69.71	11
Trinity	69.50	12
St Anne's	69.24	13
Keble	68.91	14
Oriel	68.86	15
Wadham	68.43	16
University	68.41	17
Hertford	68.14	18
St Edmund Hall	67.85	19
Exeter	67.74	20
St Peter's	67.48	21
Brasenose	67.00	22
Mansfield	66.29	23
St Catherine's	66.23	24
Harris Manchester	66.15	25
Pembroke	66.13	26
Worcester	65.87	27
Somerville	65.63	28
St Hilda's	65.18	29
Lady Margaret Hall	63.87	30

Source: The *Independent.*

each subject. There are even companies which will suggest colleges for you to target by looking at the history of competition for places. Naturally these companies will charge you a handsome fee for this service, something which you can easily do yourself. Before you go rushing to the tables in the prospectus and online, think about this . . . Although a certain college may have had only 15 applications for theology last year, how do you know that the statistics will remain the

Table 2: Tompkins Table – University of Cambridge 2008

College	Tompkins Score (%)	Firsts (%)
Selwyn	68.47	29.9
Emmanuel	68.30	30.6
Trinity	68.27	31.4
Gonville and Caius	67.33	27.9
Magdalene	65.97	24.5
Churchill	65.72	27.1
Jesus	65.60	25.2
Christ's	65.27	25.7
Corpus Christi	65.24	24.1
Pembroke	64.96	24.5
St Catharine's	64.63	23.5
Downing	64.47	22.8
Clare	64.44	22.5
Sidney Sussex	64.21	20.9
Trinity Hall	63.76	19.3
Queen's	63.58	22.3
Robinson	63.32	20.6
Peterhouse	63.21	22.9
King's	63.07	22.5
St John's	62.48	20.5
Fitzwilliam	61.08	18.2
Girton	60.84	15.3
Murray Edwards	60.02	13.9
Newnham	59.96	13.3
Homerton	58.62	13.0
Hughes Hall	56.36	20.8
Wolfson	55.13	7.4
Lucy Cavendish	52.60	8.7
St Edmund's	51.55	11.2

Source: The *Independent*.

Table 3: Permanent private hall undergraduate degree classifications
2007/2008 (sorted by rank)

PPH	Score (%)	Rank
Wycliffe Hall	65.33	1
Greyfriars	61.33	2
Blackfriars	60.00	3
Regent's Park	58.52	4
St Benet's Hall	57.78	5
St Stephen's House	53.33	6
Ripon	46.67	7

same this year when you apply? Add to that the fact that if lots of other people are paying for someone to select their college on this basis, surely the number of applications will rise, thereby making the whole process void. Don't pay too much attention to the history of entry statistics but do think carefully about some of the considerations mentioned previously. The important thing to remember is this – if you are good, you might not get into your first choice college but you also may be pooled (see page 107 for more information on pooling).

Open applications

If, after all your research, you still don't feel a particular pull to one college more than another, you can make an 'open' application. An 'open application' is one where you do not specify a college and the admissions computer will assign you to a college that is under-subscribed in your subject. If there is a college that you really do not want to go to, do not put in an 'open application' as you may get sent there and there is nothing you can do about it later. Of students getting into Oxford, 15% make 'open applications', and the success rates are the same for college-specific applications.

> If an applicant makes an open application and the statistical programme allocates that candidate to our college, the candidate will be treated as if they applied directly to our college.
>
> **Admissions Tutor, Cambridge**

Do not spend an excessive amount of time agonising over choosing a college otherwise your work may begin to suffer; if you don't get those As you won't be going to any college.

> Cooperative arrangements between the colleges are designed to ensure that able candidates applying to oversubscribed college are placed at other colleges. Almost 20% of successful candidates are placed at a college other than their college of preference each year.
>
> **Oxford Prospectus, 2008**

In any case, even though the choice of college is important, I know of nobody who has been unhappy at Oxford or Cambridge purely by virtue of being at the 'wrong' college. Wherever you end up, you are bound to settle in, make good friends and work hard.

Choosing a course

First, the emphasis at Oxford and Cambridge is on scholarship. You may be attracted by a subject because of the career prospects that it affords. That's fine. But deep interest in your subject for its own sake, and not merely as a means to an end, is vital if you are going to keep up with the workload and sustain your motivation when the intellectual demands get tough – as they should do and will.

Second, many of the pleasures to be had from your course result from making conceptual breakthroughs and seeing more in the subject than appeared at first sight. You need to be excited when you make these breakthroughs. Otherwise, you'll be missing out on one of the main benefits Oxbridge has to offer.

Third, the entire selection process at Oxford and Cambridge is much more focused on your acumen for a particular subject (as opposed to your general personality) than it is at other universities. Your aptitude is therefore crucial, but the intellectual curiosity that you display for a particular subject can help you through awkward moments in a technical interview. Admissions tutors are people too, and they can't help being positively influenced by candidates who share their passion. Such candidates tend to be more rewarding to teach.

Some people just seem to know what they want to study – their passion for the subject has been there for years. They are the lucky ones! If you are not sure then get some advice from your careers adviser or teacher. Remember not to discard subjects which you have never heard of or have not studied. Do investigate them as you may find yourself pleasantly interested. Here is an exercise to help you get started on trying to find the right course if you are not sure about your subject.

- Get hold of the prospectuses for both Oxford and Cambridge and write down all the courses they offer.
- Start by dividing the courses into lists A, B and C.
- A – courses which appear to be very different from those commonly offered at A level.
- B – courses which appear to build on some of those studied at A level.
- C – courses which appear to be simple extensions of subjects available at A level.

Note that many of these appearances may be deceptive. Here's one way of carving up the list, but it depends, of course, on what subjects are on offer to you at school. (You might, for example, wish to move psychology, computing or law from list A to list C.) We include here subjects which may be offered singly or in combination.

Oxford

List A

- Archaeology and anthropology
- Classical archaeology and ancient history
- Computer science
- Economics and management
- Experimental psychology
- Human sciences
- Law
- Oriental studies
- Philosophy
- PPE
- PPP
- Theology.

List B

- Biological sciences
- Earth sciences
- Engineering science
- Materials science
- Molecular and cellular biochemistry
- Physiological sciences and medicine.

List C

- Classics
- Chemistry
- English
- Fine art
- Geography
- History
- Mathematics
- Modern languages
- Music.

Cambridge

List A

- Anglo Saxon, Norse and Celtic studies
- Archaeology and anthropology
- Architecture
- Asian and Middle Eastern studies
- Computer science
- Education
- History of art

- Land economy
- Law
- Linguistics
- Management studies
- Philosophy
- Social and political sciences
- Theology and religious studies.

List B

- Chemical engineering
- Engineering
- Manufacturing engineering
- Medicine
- Natural sciences
- Veterinary medicine.

List C

- Classics
- Economics
- English
- Geography
- History
- Mathematics
- Modern and medieval languages
- Music.

Now have a look at the course guides in the prospectuses, paying particular attention to content and A level subject requirements. The course outlines in the prospectuses are very thorough and, whether you're familiar or unfamiliar with Oxford and Cambridge, they're your best starting point. It's remarkable how many students fall down at interview because they have not taken the trouble to find out basic information about their courses from the prospectuses.

To check that you're up to speed on these basics, critically evaluate the breakdown into lists A, B and C given above. How else could it have been carved up? What are the A level subjects that are apparently being built upon in relevant list B courses? Compare and contrast Oxford and Cambridge if you are interested in the following: biological sciences, economics, English, law, management, philosophy, physics, politics. Taking seriously what the prospectuses list as 'advantageous' (as well as 'essential') subjects at A level, start with your A level combination and list the courses at either university that appear to have an 'ideal' fit.

Get hold of more information

The next step, if you want to be more thorough, is to contact the individual faculty buildings in each university. Remember that, while the college administers the teaching, it is the faculty (i.e. the subject department within the university) that administers the syllabus. The faculty will have much more detail on course content than is available in the prospectuses. Information about faculty addresses, including website addresses, is available in the prospectuses. Cambridge applicants may also refer to *The Cambridge University Guide to Courses*, published by the Cambridge University Press.

If you're wondering if you are going to be interested in a new subject such as psychology or computing, or wondering just how much chemistry there's going to be in biological sciences or how much mathematics in chemistry, there's no substitute for putting yourself in a first-year undergraduate's shoes. Talk to any undergraduates you know. Look at their lecture notes and essays. Alternatively, get hold of reading lists from the Admissions Tutor's office at the college you have chosen to apply to and take the trouble to do some reading. Don't be afraid to ask. Even if they appear to find your request a bit odd, remember there are plenty of other people doing the same. Why not you? For all they know, you're a really strong candidate, with a thirst for extra work, who's choosing between two faculties. The worst they're going to think is that you're being incredibly thorough, and they're very unlikely to make a note of it!

You might be sent the same reading list that successful candidates are asked to work through during the summer holidays before going up to Oxford or Cambridge. That might contain some very general texts which don't relate directly to your future course work. For the first-year undergraduate texts, you might be better off contacting the faculty again. Still no luck? Take the trouble to visit the university again one Saturday and spend the afternoon in the university bookshop (Blackwell's in Oxford or Heffer's in Cambridge). The staff are very familiar with the books that are used by undergraduates.

Changing subjects

Having said all of that, it may be that you end up choosing the wrong subject, but don't realise this until you get to university. Or, you may wish to study more than one subject. At Oxford, you apply for your subject and normally students continue to study that subject for the duration of their time at university. That is not to say that the focus is narrow, there are many options within your subject you can choose and options increase as you go from year to year. Also it is not unheard of to change subjects after your first year, provided you have a good reason, have passed your first-year exams and can demonstrate a deep interest in and commitment to your new subject. Changing subjects is at the discretion of your college.

At Cambridge there is a more formalised approach to changing subjects and perhaps a wider recognition that students may change their mind about what they want to study or a recognition that students may want to study more than one subject that may or may not be related to each other. This is the Tripos system (see page 11). Most students go to Cambridge and think they want to study one subject. If, after a year, they want to change their subject, for example, to law, they have to notify their college and then join a two-year law course specially designed for people who have changed subjects. The three-year law degree has been crammed into two years so it is hard work, but you graduate in law just as someone who studies law from the beginning of their degree would graduate. In fact, you can only take certain subjects such as linguistics, chemical engineering, manufacturing engineering and history and philosophy of science at Part II level; you cannot apply for these for your first-year course. A small number of students may apply to Cambridge and already know that they want to do one year of one subject and then change to another subject. If they are confident that they can show commitment to both subjects and can justify why they want to do it, they should write their intentions on the Supplementary Application Questionnaire. You may come out of Cambridge with two Part Is in two subjects, a Part I and a Part II in two related subjects or a Part I and a Part II in unrelated subjects. It very much depends on the subjects you choose. You will not be disadvantaged by not knowing what you want to do in Part II and if you change your mind later on – that is fine.

Checklist

- Research course content in prospectuses.
- Analyse fit with A levels.
- Contact faculties.
- Talk to current undergraduates.
- Get hold of the reading lists.
- Visit the bookshops.

02 Entry requirements

Qualifications

In order to apply to Oxford or Cambridge you will need excellent marks at A level or the International Baccalaureate, Scottish Highers or any other qualification that Oxford or Cambridge accepts. You will also need excellent grades in your GCSEs or your country's equivalent qualification. Typically a good candidate will take eight to 10 GCSEs with around five or six of them at A*. The subjects are less important in the case of GCSE than A levels and you have probably already taken your GCSEs at this point. If you haven't, then in addition to English (language and/or literature), maths and science, I can recommend doing the following:

- at least one language
- at least one humanities subject (geography, history or religious studies)
- you don't need to but you could do a practical subject, for example, art, ICT (information and communication technology), design technology (clearly if you want to apply to Oxford to read fine art you will need to do art and if you want to do computer science you may opt to do ICT).

If you follow this you will have a broad foundation for your A levels or further qualifications, enabling you to take any subject at A level. If you do not take a range of GCSEs, you will be limiting your choices at A level. It is also important to show that at this foundation level, you are an all-rounder.

Alternatives to A levels in the UK

There have been some recent changes and additions to the qualifications available in the UK and it may be that you are not sure whether what you are studying will be acceptable. Neither university favours one qualification over another as they appreciate that you have no choice as to which examination system you are under. The main qualifications which might apply to you and which you may be unsure about are explained below. After each description, I have added a synopsis of the universities' stance.

Cambridge Pre-U

Cambridge Pre-U is a post-16 qualification designed to prepare students with the skills and knowledge they need to be successful at university. It challenges students to show not only a keen grasp of their subject, but also lateral, critical and contextual thinking. It encourages individual, independent research and promotes learning through innovative approaches to curriculum and assessment. Students may take individual Cambridge Pre-U subjects. There are 26 available. However, if they successfully study three principal subjects, in combination with completing an individual research report and compiling a global perspectives portfolio, over two years, they will be awarded the Cambridge Pre-U Diploma.

Cambridge Pre-U is a two-year programme of study. The structure of each Cambridge Pre-U syllabus is linear, so students take exams at the end of the whole course. Both universities will accept the Pre-U but express no preference for it over any other qualification.

The extended project

The extended project is a separate qualification that A level students may add to their study programme. Students carry out a project on a topic of their own choosing which may or may not be linked to their chosen A level subjects. The projects involve planning, research and evaluation, but the end product students produce may be a dissertation, the findings of an investigation or field study, a performance or an artefact. The aim of the extended project is to develop research and independent learning skills that will be of great benefit in higher education and employment.

Currently neither university uses the extended project in its offers, but they recognise the benefits it can have in terms of the skills it can develop in students, skills which can ease the transition from secondary to higher education. Cambridge has stated that the extended project may be a suitable topic for discussion at interview and in some cases, where it is relevant, it may be an appropriate piece of written work to be submitted.

The Diploma

Specialised Diplomas are new qualifications for 14–19-year-olds. They have been created to provide an alternative to more traditional education and qualifications, and are the most important change to the UK's education system since the introduction of GCSEs. A diploma is an all-round package which gives students the right knowledge, experience, insight and attitude to prepare them for the next stage in life – whether that's university, college or work. There are different levels of diploma, with the most appropriate one for a potential university applicant being the Advanced Diploma. This is the equivalent of 3.5 A levels.

Both Oxford and Cambridge will accept the Advanced Diploma in Engineering for applicants to their engineering courses. Note, though, that you will also need to include both A level Physics and the Level 3 Certificate in Mathematics for Engineering. Both universities have made no statement so far on their acceptance of other diploma subjects. ·

I don't have five or six A*s at GCSE

There may be several reasons for this. Perhaps you are a late academic bloomer or you have only just started taking your studies seriously. If you fall into either of these categories, as long as you go the extra mile or hundred miles at the A level stage you may still be in with a chance (see later). However, if you are reading this book in your GCSE year, or before, the best thing you can do is to work really hard with a good study regime and do really well in your GCSEs.

It may, however, be that you were unwell or, for some other reason, unable to commit fully to your studies. Both Oxford and Cambridge are sympathetic to unusual and/or difficult situations so it is vital that you are honest with them about your reasons.

Cambridge Special Access Scheme

If you are in the above situation with good reason, you may like to consider making an application under the Special Access Scheme at Cambridge. The main function of the scheme is to focus on the problems faced by those who do not have a history of applying to university. If nobody from your family and very few people from your school have gone to university in the past, then you will be eligible to apply. You can also apply if your education has been 'significantly disrupted or disadvantaged through health or personal problems, disability or difficulties with schooling'. If you do apply through this scheme, your school will be asked to provide a far fuller reference than normal, so it is important that you talk things through with a teacher first.

A levels

If you are lucky enough to go to a very supportive school, you will probably get a lot of guidance about your A level choices, particularly in light of the fact that you are thinking of applying to Oxford or Cambridge. If you are not so lucky, then don't worry, this book will help you make the right decision.

First of all, you need to acknowledge that there is a 'currency' in A levels. An A level in Media Studies is not (rightly or wrongly) worth the same as an A level in Chemistry.

'Unacceptable' or 'soft-option' A levels

There has been extensive news coverage about 'soft option' A levels, which describes research into the comparability of an A and an E grade in different subjects. It has been suggested by some that it is easier to get an A in some subjects than in others. In response to this, Cambridge once compiled a list of A level subjects that together, it considers to be less effective preparation for its courses and would therefore probably only include in an offer as a third subject. This list has however, been very recently withdrawn. However, I would advise that if one of the subjects you really want to study is in the list below, make sure it is your fourth A level and do not do more than one.

Cambridge list of 'unacceptable' A levels

- Accounting
- Art and Design (may be acceptable in some cases – check architecture requirements, this also varies between colleges: some colleges accept art as an academic A level and some do not; of course for fine art at Oxford it is acceptable)
- Business Studies
- Communication Studies
- Dance
- Design and Technology (may be acceptable in some cases – check engineering requirements)
- Drama/Theatre Studies (may be acceptable in some cases – check education and English requirements (Cambridge only))
- Film Studies
- General Studies (as a fourth A level only)
- Health and Social Care
- Home Economics
- Information and Communication Technology
- Leisure Studies
- Media Studies
- Music Technology
- Performance Studies
- Performing Arts

- Photography
- Physical Education
- Sports Studies
- Travel and Tourism

To be a realistic applicant, a student will normally need to be offering two traditional academic subjects (i.e. two subjects not on the 'unacceptable list')... For students studying for the International Baccalaureate not more than one of the subjects listed should be taken a higher level to count as part of the Diploma.
Cambridge admissions webpages

How may As?

You should be predicted to get three or four As at A level. Due to the competitive nature of A levels now, it is not enough to get three or four As at the end, you need to get very high scores in the majority of the individual modules that make up the AS and A2. As a rough guide, you should know that the majority of sccessful applicants achieve around 90% in each module. Also be aware that in 2010, A*s for A level are going to be introduced to differentiate the best from the good. At Cambridge the standard offer will now be A*AA, with offers for science degrees likely to specify the subject in which the A* should be achieved. Oxford, however, does not plan to request A* grades at the moment.

The degree of flexibility in your A level subject choice will depend to an extent on which course you apply to. For example, if you are going to apply for medicine at Cambridge then you will need three of the following at A level: chemistry, physics, maths and biology (chemistry must be a full A level). Although some subjects require specific subjects to be taken, some courses require no specific A levels, just A grades in them and a proven interest in the subject to be studied at university. It is important that you can justify your subject choice and that the choice seems coherent. You need to make sure that you come across as a student who plans things carefully.

When looking at your A level choices we ask ourselves whether the student has the intellectual and academic training to get through the first part of the Tripos.
Admissions Tutor, Cambridge

Subjects that do not require a specific A level subject are:

- Anglo-Saxon, Norse and Celtic
- archaeology and anthropology
- classical archaeology and ancient history

- classics (four years – Cambridge)
- law
- geography (Cambridge – at Oxford they do want Geography A level)
- history of art
- human sciences
- land economy (Cambridge)
- law
- oriental sciences
- philosophy (Cambridge)
- philosophy and theology
- PPE (Oxford)
- SPS (Cambridge)
- theology.

If you have little idea about what you want to study at this stage, I would recommend studying the subjects you know that you enjoy. No matter how tough they may be, you are more likely to get good grades if you actually enjoy what you are studying. If you are mathematically able, maths is always a good bet as it can increase your options of subjects you can apply for at university. Similarly, choosing an essay writing-based subject such as history or English is a good idea. If you want to take a science, chemistry is the science that links together all the other sciences and will form a solid basis for many degrees, particularly in conjunction with maths. In addition, languages are always an asset for jobs as well as for university. If you are weighing up two options of courses make sure you are taking the required subjects for both if possible. In the worst case scenario, if you realise you have chosen the wrong subject, you could sit the A level the next year at a tutorial college or buy the books, read round the subject and try learning it yourself.

How many A levels?

Conditional offers from both universities are likely to be A*AA–AAA so you must take at least three courses to A2 level. They would both expect you to have done four AS levels as well.

Tips for getting those As – revision and hard work

A levels are very different now from what they used to be. You are probably taking exams in the January and June of both your A level years. This means that you need to be on top of your work and revision at all times. In order to achieve the highest grades you must work very hard constantly. This means going to see your teacher in your break if you did not understand the work in class. When revising for your A level modules, I would advise buying some A level study guides. Go to a bookshop or your local library and browse their school section. Pick a subject you know well and see how the book explains it. If it explains it well, then it may well explain other topics well. I would recommend buying two different study guides per subject so that if you cannot follow one, you can use the other to get a different perspective. Many study guides have past exam questions which you can attempt and check the answers in the back. If you get an answer wrong, then go back to the question and see if you can work it out. If you are really stumped, then take the question to your teacher. Your teacher will be delighted that you are taking your studies seriously so do not worry about bombarding him/her with questions! The key is to show him/her that you have tried the question twice.

At A level it is often important to learn definitions or chains of events. Write them out and compare them with the definition in the textbook or study guide until you can do it perfectly. Your teachers may be giving you lots of past paper practice and letting you see the mark schemes. It is important to look at the mark schemes as it enables you to see directly what the examiner is looking for. If your teacher is not giving you many papers, then ask them to. Increasingly, the exam boards are putting past papers and mark schemes on the internet. The main examination board web addresses are as follows:

- Oxford Cambridge and RSA Examinations (OCR): www.ocr.org.uk
- Assessment and Qualifications Alliance (AQA): www.aqa.org.uk
- Edexcel: www.edexcel.org.uk

For other exam boards type their name into a search engine such as Google, select the qualification you are studying for and navigate to the past paper materials. It is also important to make sure you know what information you are meant to learn. Your teacher may have given you a copy of the syllabus – if not, it can be downloaded from the exam board's website – it is referred to as the 'specification'. Check the exam code with your teacher first in case there is more than one specification.

As you get nearer the exams, you will have to make sure that in addition to your usual study routine, you factor in revision time for after you come home from school. I suggest making a revision timetable for the two-month run-up to the exams listing every day you have until the exams, including weekends, so that you can plan your revision. After school, when you have done your homework you should spend two hours doing revision. The most important thing is to make sure your revision is effective. Staring into space for two hours does not count as revision. At the end of each evening arrange the books ready for the next evening so that when you begin your revision session fresh and awake you do not have to waste valuable time sorting out where your books are.

Revision technique is a personal thing and you have probably already got plenty of ideas of how you work best, if you have done well in your GCSEs. The key point is that in some subjects you need to learn lots of information. Reading the information through is not enough – you need to do something active with it. Try rewriting it in bullet point form or in a flow chart. Cover up the bullet points and try writing it again by heart. Draw out diagrams without looking at the original and then compare them with the original. Highlight any mistakes and draw them out again. Write out equations or reactions. Attempt a maths question for which you have a model answer, compare your stages of answers with theirs and see where you went wrong. Do the question again until you get it right. And most importantly of all, test yourself regularly. Try writing out a test on the topic before you start revising it.

Have a rest after 45–50 minutes. This is your break – do not be tempted to start watching TV or going on MSN. Go back up to your study room and continue. When you do your next revision session, start by drawing out the diagrams and flow charts from the previous session without looking at your notes. You should be building up a bank of diagrams and flowcharts. You could put these on cards or just make your own notebook to refer to on the day of the exams – this should be a very concise summary.

It is important when you do your revision that your mobile phone is switched off and you are not on Facebook. Two hours of emailing does not count as two hours of revision. If you put in the work now, then you will reap the rewards later. The important thing to get into your head is that you will not have much of a social life while you are revising. But do not worry, this is a temporary stage in your life and it is a means to an end. If you get those grades and get to a good university, hopefully Oxford or Cambridge, then your social life will be great when you get there.

When you know the dates and times of your exams, draw up a timetable and pin it on your wall. Make sure you write down how long each exam is, how many questions there are and based on the marks allocated to each section, how long each section should take you. Your teacher should be able to help you on this. It is important to make sure you have sorted out this basic strategy well in advance of your exam.

Dealing with stress

All this revision can easily become stressful, so it is important to listen to your feelings. If you are exhausted, then the best thing you can do is go to bed or perhaps take a day off from studying at the weekend. There are many effects of stress, including sleeplessness and headaches, tearfulness, loneliness, excessive eating or not eating enough. If you feel that you are suffering from these or similar symptoms, then try talking to a friend or your parents about it. It may be that they can offer you some perspective. Perhaps you have a school counsellor you can see, or if not go and see your GP. Studying for A levels is hard and many students are in a similar position.

Some practical measures you can take if you are feeling stressed or feel unable to get down to work are to change your work routine. You may find that you prefer to do your two hours of studying before school and not at night. Perhaps you would benefit from studying with a friend once in a while. Studying is an isolating process and it is important to build social activities into your timetable to keep yourself sane. Make sure you do some form of exercise regularly and are eating balanced and healthy meals.

Checklist

- Check the A level subject requirements for your course(s).
- When choosing your A levels, remember that too many non-traditional subjects may affect your chances of an offer.
- Don't worry if your school does not offer A levels. Check what the subject requirements are for equivalent qualifications.

03 Preparing to apply

Once you have decided to apply and you know which subject you would like to read, you need to start planning your application. In an ideal world, you will have decided on your application several months in advance. Some students know for years that they are going to apply to Oxbridge, but realistically we can't all be that organised or that sure of ourselves so early on in life. You will probably have a good idea that you will applying when you are half way through your Lower Sixth year. This will give you plenty of time to organise work experience (for advice on this, see below). You will also have time to get reading around your subject and research your chosen degree course. Here are some of my suggestions as to how to get yourself prepared to make a good application.

Taking help from teachers

Tell your teachers that you are going to apply! It's important to have their support and for them to know that you are aiming high in your A levels. It will also help them to know that at some point you may have to send in marked work to the university as part of your application.

Ask a teacher who is a specialist in the subject for which you are applying if they can suggest some reading that you ought to do. You are not expected to read undergraduate textbooks, but you should be looking to try to understand a little more about the subject than you already know. Once you've read the book(s) it is important to go back to your teacher and discuss it with him or her just to ensure that you have understood it. As well as books your teacher may recommend, you might like to browse a bookstore for subject-related books. For example, you might enjoy reading a biography about someone who was/is famous in the field in which you are interested. This all adds to your own knowledge and gives you more to mention in your application.

Events around you

Try to find events near you which are related to your subject. For example, a local library may host a talk by an author. Other places will give talks on specific subjects. For example, you could look at the Royal Institute and the Science Museum for science lectures, the Royal Geographic Society for geography lectures. Local universities may hold talks as well. Speak to your teacher for ideas or go online to a search engine and try typing in your subject name alongside the words 'talk' or 'lecture' and the name of your town or city. Other things you could try to do are:

- for politics – go on a tour of the Houses of Parliament
- for law – sit in the public gallery of your local magistrate's or Crown court
- for history and archaeology – visit the British Museum
- for art and history of art – go to the galleries local to Oxford and Cambridge if you can, as this will show a real interest not only in your subject but also quite clearly in the towns themselves. Clearly, however, any gallery visit will be beneficial and enjoyable.

Things you have done or achieved

Next, you should write down all the things of note you have done in recent years. Perhaps you have travelled to interesting countries, volunteered for an organisation, gone to a summer school, won academic prizes or competitions. The reason for doing this as soon as you have decided to apply is so that you can store the list somewhere safe to refer to when you make your application. It's amazing how quickly we forget the good things we have done, so I recommend keeping this list.

Along with that list, you ought to start thinking about your application and how you are going to convince Oxford or Cambridge that you are a worthy candidate. Your first chance to do this is in the Personal Statement, which is discussed in detail later in the book. For the moment, you need to think about the bare bones of that statement. Here are some questions that you may like to consider.

- What or who made you become interested in your subject?
- How can you demonstrate that you have followed up your interest?
- Have you read any interesting books?
- How can you demonstrate that you are able to commit to something (the admissions tutor will want evidence that you have enough tenacity to stick at the course and that you will be an asset to the college), for example, volunteering, work experience, etc.
- Have you taken part in activities in your school, for example debating, school newspaper, drama, choir or set up a society/club?

Getting to know your subject better

Here I have given some suggestions for ways in which you can 'read around' your subject. The list is by no means exhaustive and is *not* a list of books you *must* read, just some suggestions about the types of things you should be reading. Many thanks to James Burnett and the departmental heads of MPW for their help in compiling this list.

Economics/management

- *The Writing on the Wall: China and the West in the 21st Century*, Will Hutton
- *Making Globalisation Work*, Joseph Stiglitz
- *Poor Story (Globalisation)*, Giles Bolton
- *The Corporation*, Joel Bakn
- *The Google Story*, David A. Wise
- *Swimming Against the Stream*, Tim Waterstone
- *The Starbucks Experience*, Joseph Michelli
- *Myself and Other Important Matters*, Charles Handy
- *How They Started*, David Lester
- *Good to Great*, Jim Collins
- *The Long Tail*, Chris Anderson
- *The Dragon and the Elephant (India and China)*, David Smith
- *Capitalism*, Jonathan Porritt
- *How Rich Countries Got Rich*, Eric S. Reinhart
- *Freakonomics*, S. Levitt and S. Dubner
- *Globalisation and its Discontents*, Joseph Stiglitz
- *Fooled by Randomness*, Nasim Nicholas Talib
- *China Shakes the World*, James Kynge
- *The Undercover Economist*, Tim Harford
- *Confessions of an Economic Hit Man*, John Perkins

English

If you have a favourite author or authors and you declare this in your Personal Statement, be sure to have read as much of their work as possible. Know your author as well as their works. Investigate them as people, rather than only appreciating their writing. In addition, the following books are interesting works.

- *The Soul of the Age: Life, Mind and World of William Shakespeare*, Jonathan Bate
- *Literary Theory: A Very Short Introduction*, Jonathan Culler
- *Structuralist Poetics*, Jonathan Culler
- *On Deconstruction: Theory and Criticism after Structuralism*, Jonathan Culler

- *Critical Approaches to English Literature*, David Daiches
- *Beginning Theory: An Introduction to Literary and Cultural Theory*, Peter Barry
- *Literary Theory: An Introduction*, Terry Eagleton
- *Shakespeare: The Thinker*, A. D. Nuttall
- *Why Does Tragedy Give Pleasure?*, A. D. Nuttall
- *Revenge Tragedy: From Aeschylus to Armageddon*, John Kerrigan

History

The key piece of advice for would-be Oxbridge historians is to ensure that they have read widely about their A level topics. They need to show an awareness of recent historical debate and to understand different interpretations. The books listed below either deal with historiography or are (in my view) particularly well written and deserving of attention.

- *The Historian's Craft*, Marc Bloch
- *History and Social Theory*, Peter Burke
- *What is History?*, E. H. Carr
- *The Practice of History*, Geoffrey Elton
- *In Defence of History*, Richard J. Evans
- *The Pursuit of History*, John Tosh
- *In Churchill's Shadow*, David Cannadine
- *Roundhead Reputations*, Blair Worden
- *Dark Continent: Europe's Twentieth Century*, Mark Mazower
- *Pursuit of Glory*, Tim Blanning

Law

- *The Juryman's Tale*, Trevor Grove
- *The Magistrate's Tale*, Trevor Grove
- *Learning the Law*, Glanville Williams
- *The New Penguin Guide to the Law*, John Pritchard
- *The Law Machine*, Marcel Berlins and Clare Dyer
- *The Politics of the Judiciary*, J. A. G. Griffith
- *The Discipline of Law*, Lord Denning
- *McLibel: Burger Culture on Trial*, John Vidal

Medicine

- *Aspirin*, Diarmuid Jeffreys
- *Body Story*, Dr David Wilham
- *Catching Cold*, Pete Davies and Michael Joseph
- *Don't Die Young*, Dr Alice Roberts
- *Everything You Need to Know about Bird Flu*, Jo Revill

- *How We Die*, Sherwin Nuland
- *How We Live*, Sherwin Nuland
- *The Human Brain: A Guided Tour*, Susan Greenfield
- *Practical Medical Ethics*, David Seedhouse and Lisetta Lovett
- *The Trouble with Medicine*, Dr Melvin Konner
- *Stop the 21st Century Killing You*, Dr Paula Bailie-Hamilton

Modern languages

French
Reading

- *Le Misanthrope*, Molière
- *Maximes*, La Rochefoucauld
- *Candide ou Micromegas (très court)*, Voltaire
- *Trois Contes*, Flaubert
- *La Chute*, Camus
- *La Clé sur la Porte*, Marie Cardinal
- *La Porte Étroite*, A. Gide
- *Sur la Lecture*, Proust

Films

See films by Truffaut, Robert Bresson, André Téchiné, Eric Rohmer and Louis Malle [ses films français] and read the following texts if possible:

- *Les films de Ma Vie* (Truffaut)
- *Notes sur le cinématographe* (Bresson)

German
Reading

- *Die Verlorene Ehre der Katharina Blum*, Heinrich Böll
- *Mutter Courage; Kaukasischer Kreidekreis*, Bertolt Brecht
- *Die Physiker; Der Besuch der alten Dame*, Friedrich Dürrenmatt
- *Andorra*, Max Frisch
- *Die Blechtrommel; Katz und Maus*, Gunther Grass
- *Die Verwandlung; Sämtliche Erzählungen*, Franz Kafka
- *Tonio Kröger; Der Tod in Venedig*, Thomas Mann
- *Der Vorleser*, Bernhard Schlink (the book, not the film!)
- *Das Parfum; Die Taube*, Patrick Süskind
- *Ideology of the Aesthetic; Literary Theory*, Terry Eagleton (for articles on psychoanalytic literary theory)

Art

Taschen books are easily available and cheap. Read in English or German.

- Expressionism
- Bauhaus
- Wiener Werkstätte

Films about the Second World War

- *Sophie Scholl*
- *Der Untergang*
- *Die Faelscher*
- *Europa, Europa*
- *Das Boot*
- *Heimat*

Films about the former East Germany

- *Goodbye Lenin!*
- *Sonnenallee*
- *Der Tunnel*
- *Leben der Anderen*
- *Der Himmel über Berlin*

General films

- *Lola Rennt*
- *Gegen die Wand*
- *Das Experiment*
- *Die Apothekerin*
- *Napola*
- *Angst essen Seele auf*
- *Die Ehe der Maria Braun*
- *The American Friend*
- *Alice in den Städten*

Italian

- *Se questo è un uomo*, Primo Levi
- *Lessico famigliare*, Natalia Ginzburg
- *Se una notte d'inverno un viaggiatore*, Italo Calvino
- *A ciascuno il suo*, Leonardo Sciascia
- *Il gattopardo*, Tomasi di Lampedusa
- *La coscienza di Zeno*, Italo Svevo
- *Sei Personaggi in Cerca d'Autore*, Pirandello

Russian

- *One Day in the Life of Ivan Denisovich*, Aleksandr Solzhenitsyn
- *Anna Karenina*, Lev Tolstoy
- *Uncle Vanya*, Anton Chekhov
- *The Brothers Karamazov*, Fyodor Dostoevsky

- *A Month in the Country*, Ivan Turgenev
- *Doctor Zhivago*, Boris Pasternak
- *The Master and Margarita*, Mikhail Bulgakov
- *Eugene Onegin*, Alexander Pushkin
- *A Hero of our Time*, Mıkhaıl Lermontov
- *Requiem*, Anna Akhmatova
- *Collected Poems in English, 1972–1999*, Iosif Brodsky
- *Taras Bul'ba*, Nikolai Gogol
- *Life of Arseniev*, Ivan Bunin

Spanish
Reading

- *La Celestina*, Fernando de Rojas
- *La Vida es Sueño*, Pedro Calderón de la Barca
- *El Quijote*, Miguel de Cervantes
- *La Regenta*, Leopoldo Alas
- *El Árbol de la Ciencia*, Pio Baroja
- *La Tía Tula*, Miguel de Unamuno
- *El Surrealismo y Cuatro Poetas de la Generación del 27: (Ensayo Sobre Extensión y Límites del Surrealismo en la Generación del 27)*, Carlos Marcial
- *Poeta en Nueva York; La Casa de Bernarda Alba*, Federico García Lorca
- *La Familia de Pascual Duarte; La Colmena*, Camilo José Cela
- *Tiempo de Silencio*, Luis Martin-Santos
- *Señas de Identidad*, Juan Goytisolo
- *La Ciudad de los Prodigios*, Eduardo Mendoza
- *Corazón Tan Blanco*, Javier Marías
- *Cien Años de Soledad*, Gabriel García Márquez
- *La Ciudad y los Perros*, Mario Vargas Llosa
- *Rayuela*, Julio Cortázar
- *Confieso Que he Vivido*, Pablo Neruda
- *Cinco Horas con Mario*, Miguel Delibes
- *El Jarama*, Rafael Sánchez Ferlosio
- *Lo Raro es Vivir*, Carmen Martin Gaite
- *Olvidado Rey Gudú*, Ana María Matute

Films

- *Todo Sobre mi Madre*, Pedro Almodóvar
- *La Caza; Cría Cuervos; Elisa, Vida mía*, Carlos Saura
- *El Espíritu de la Colmena*, Víctor Erice
- *Iñárritu Amores Perros*, Alejandro González
- *Las Bicicletas son Para el Verano*, Jaime Chávarri

Psychology

- *Body Language*, Allan Pease
- *Emotional Intelligence*, Daniel Goleman
- *Mapping the Mind*, Rita Carter
- *Memory*, David Samuel
- *Phobias – Fighting the Fear*, Helen Saul
- *The Human Mind*, Robert Winston
- *Totem and Talent*, Sigmund Freud

Science/engineering/maths

- Any book by Einstein
- *Black Bodies and Quantum Cats*, Jennifer Ouellette
- *The Equation that Couldn't be Solved*, Mario Livio
- *Dr Riemann's Zeros*, Karl Sabbagh
- *Zero*, Charles Seife
- *Fermat's Last Theorem*, Simon Singh
- *Critical Mass*, Philip Ball
- *Genesis Machines*, Martyn Amos
- *Chaos*, James Glick
- *The Elegant Universe*, Brian Greene
- *How Long is a Piece of String?*, Rob Eastaway and Jeremy Wyndham
- *The Infinite Book*, John D. Barrow

Work experience

You may not have had any work experience. It is important to try to get some work experience, not only to show commitment for the purposes of the UCAS form (i.e. if you are committed enough to hold down a job and do well in it, you will also be committed enough to finish your degree and get the most out of it) but also because it is very helpful later on in life when you are deciding what sort of job you would like to do. For example, you may get work experience in some kind of office and realise that office work is not for you. You may shadow a barrister and think that you can see yourself doing that as a career. Getting work experience can sometimes be tricky and you have to implement several strategies at the same time. This includes asking all your relatives and getting your parents to ask their friends if you can go to work with them for a week or more; asking your school if they have links with your local community and whether they can set up some work experience. You can also visit your local Connexions office (Connexions is a government-run organisation that helps young people make career decisions) and you can also write/email or telephone organisations directly and ask if you can get some work experience or volunteer. The organisation may ask for a reference from your teacher and you will have to ask them if they are happy to write a reference for you. Perhaps it Is becoming clear that your teacher plays a very important role in your university application – not only directly in terms of writing your university reference but also indirectly, as they will write your reference for work experience, if necessary, which is important for your Personal Statement.

Organising work experience or volunteering can take several weeks or months, so make sure you do this well in advance of your AS level summer. Remember, any type of work experience is fine.

What you gain from the work experience is more valuable than the actual work experience. It can be just as valuable making tea in a hospice as shadowing a consultant in a top hospital. It shows just as much commitment working every Saturday in a supermarket as being an Olympic swimmer.

Admissions Tutor, Cambridge

Getting work experience

Below is a sample letter you could send to find some work experience. The words in italics need to be adapted as appropriate for your situation. There are some important points to note.

- When you write a letter, if you know the name of the person to whom it is addressed you must sign off 'Yours sincerely'; if you do not know the name of the person and you write 'Dear Sir/Madam' or 'To whom it may concern', then you must sign off 'Yours faithfully'.
- It is much better to write the person's name rather than write a generic 'To whom it may concern', so make a phone call and find out who deals with work experience or who the human resources manager is. If you are writing a letter to a contact, then address the letter directly to them.
- Whether you ask for work experience or to shadow someone depends on their profession. If they are a barrister or a doctor it would be best to shadow them, which means following them throughout the week and attending everything they attend. If you are applying to work in a business then you should ask for work experience, as you could be given a project to do and really demonstrate your skills (which you can then write about in your Personal Statement!).

- It is important to organise your work experience well in advance (at least three months), as businesses and organisations are inundated with requests for work experience.
- The 'Enc. CV' at the bottom lets the reader know that as well as the letter you have enclosed a document, in this case your curriculum vitae (CV).
- Your school should help you write your CV, and there are many books and websites around to help you. As a quick guide I have included a sample CV.
- It is much more efficient to email your work experience letter and CV. When you call up the business or organisation ask if they have an email address you can send it to. If you do send it in email form you do not need to write your address, their address or the date. Just start 'Dear Mr Bloggs'.
- If you do not hear back after a week to 10 days, you should email them again or perhaps call and explain that you sent them an email about work experience a few days ago and have not heard anything. Perhaps they didn't receive it.
- You ought to apply for lots of work experience at a number of companies, as not every organisation offers these opportunities and places will be limited. The more you apply for, the greater your chances of getting a good placement, or possibly even two. If you do get offered two placements, do them both. The more varied experiences you have the more you have to write about.
- On the last day of your work experience, hand in a thank you letter, using the model letter below and ask if they are happy to write a reference to send to your teacher, both in the letter and verbally. This is crucial, as your teacher can incorporate comments in their reference about you. The more you help your teacher out the better the reference will be. An example of a reference from an employer is given below.

Sample letter requesting work experience placement

Mr Joe Bloggs MP	Your address
The House of Commons	Your telephone number
Westminster	Your email address
London SW1	
Date	

Dear Mr Bloggs,
I would very much like to *undertake some work experience in your office/shadow you for a week* because I am very interested

in exploring a *career in politics*. I am currently studying for my A levels in *Spanish, Maths and Chemistry* at *Green Fields School* and I have *enclosed/attached* my CV. My summer holiday commences on *July 14 and continues until August 16*. I very much hope that you will be able to fit a week in sometime between those dates. Please could you contact me at the address or email given above at your convenience. I look forward to hearing from you.

Yours sincerely,

Your signature
Your name
Enc. CV

I wanted to get some work experience in the media business but had no contacts. I wrote letters to 15 organisations 'cold'. Ten never got back to me, four were unable to take me on as they had other work experience students and one offered me a week's work experience. I would definitely apply to many organisations at the same time.

Oxford Applicant

Sample thank you letter

Mr Joe Bloggs MP
The House of Commons
Westminster
London SW1
Date

Your address
Your telephone number
Your email address

Dear Mr Bloggs,
Thank you so much for showing me around the House of Commons on Tuesday, and for letting me work in your office this week. I really enjoyed it – especially being allowed to watch the House of Commons debate. I was wondering if you would be so kind as to write a reference about me and send it to my teacher at Green Fields School, Ealing, London, WO OAA.

Thank you very much again.

Yours sincerely

Your signature
Your name

A sample CV

At this stage of your life, you may feel that there is little to write on your CV. However, the CV is a useful document to enclose with your work experience letter as it gives the employer some useful basic information and the final section of 'interests and activities' adds a bit of colour. The format of CVs varies considerably, but a general rule of thumb is that they must not exceed two A4 pages in length, they must be word processed and not handwritten and they must be easy on the eye to read.

You must be able to back up anything you write on your CV, just like your Personal Statement. Put down any work experience you have, including babysitting, as the new employer may want some form of reference for you. If you have absolutely no work experience, you could ask your teacher to write a reference for you. You should constantly update your CV. When you have some work experience under your belt, remember to add it to your CV as well as using it in your Personal Statement. You will find that when you come to apply for jobs after university, your work experience will still be very useful. These model letters will be helpful when you are applying for internships in your summer vacations too!

Example CV

Josephine Bloggs
Your address
Nationality: British
Date of Birth: 7 February 1990
Tel: 01865 777 777
Mobile: 07765 123 456
Email: myemail@email.com

Education

Secondary: Green Fields School, London (2001–2008)
Three A levels: Spanish, Chemistry, Maths (grades pending)
Ten GCSEs: French, Latin, Spanish, Dual Award Science, English Language, English Literature, History, Computer Studies (all grade A* except Maths – grade A)

Skills

- Can explain ideas clearly and concisely (presentations at school)
- Excellent public speaking skills (debated competitively for school)
- Inter-personal skills
- Negotiation and organisational skills (founded and chaired charity committee)
- Analysis
- Won prize for ICT GCSE project write-up which tested a system I devised
- Research and writing
- Commended for research and writing skills in Spanish essay
- Computation
- Skilled in Microsoft Word, Excel, Internet Explorer, Power Point

Work experience

- Babysitting (July 2007)
- Newspaper round, Green Field (January 2006–January 2007)
- Newsagent, London

Interests and activities

- Part of the netball team
- Enjoy cooking
- Enjoy going to the theatre

References

Your teacher will probably have to write many references. How can you help her (and thus help yourself) to write a good reference? The first thing you can do is to make sure that you have regular contact with your teacher. Make sure they know who you are and how nice you are. Are you someone who has a 100% attendance rate and about whom teachers never have a complaint in? Have you discussed your application with your teacher? Do they know the things that you have accomplished lower down the school? Are they aware of your proudest achievements?

Example of an employer reference after shadowing a professional

Georgina spent a week with us at the National Hospital for Neurology on a work placement. During that time she closely observed the work of physicians, surgeons and nurses as they cared for inpatients and outpatients. Georgina is clearly committed to a career in medicine and has an advanced and realistic understanding of its demands. Our impression was that Georgina, as well as being very academic, has excellent empathetic and social skills. She was very enthusiastic about the time she spent with us and will make an excellent doctor. She was at all times punctual and reliable and her pleasant manner both with staff and patients was of specific note. Her interest, enthusiasm and intelligence bode well for her as she follows her desired path of interest in medicine. I have no hesitation in recommending her for placement in medical school.

Example of an employer reference after volunteering over a sustained period of time

Georgina has volunteered at the hospice for a year and is a most valuable member of the team of volunteers. She is dedicated and committed, doing regular shifts here. Georgina has been very dependable and reliable, proving that she can handle awkward and sometimes potentially upsetting situations with great tact and maturity. Despite having a busy study schedule Georgina has volunteered her own precious spare time at weekends – and given invaluable service to the hospice. It is always a pleasure to see her and her enthusiasm is infectious.

Georgina is very popular with members of staff and other volunteers alike. Patients, who in many instances are extremely ill, especially appreciate seeing a friendly and familiar face

These would both be incredibly helpful to your teacher in writing your reference, as they help to explain how you behave in a non-academic environment as well.

What happens if you think that for some reason your teacher will be writing a negative reference?

If you feel that the reference your teacher is going to write may put you at a disadvantage, you need to ask yourself why this may be the case. Remember that your teachers are genuinely concerned to ensure that you achieve your goals if they are realistic. They are therefore willing to do all that they can to help you out. If you understand that your reference may not be positive, talk to the teacher writing the reference and find out precisely why. You may find that they do not believe that your application is realistic, in which case, go and convince them otherwise. Hopefully you should not get to this point because, if you made the decision to apply to Oxbridge well in advance, you will hopefully have had many months to impress all of your teachers.

Checklist

- Start doing some activities to prove you are interested in your subject.
- Start applying for work experience early, as it may take several months to organise and you have to persevere.
- Cultivate a good relationship with the person who is going to write your reference for you early on.
- Ask your work experience employer to send a reference directly to your teacher (and it does no harm to ask for a copy to be sent to you as well).

04 The application

This chapter is going to focus on the nuts and bolts of the application process. The process for Oxbridge changed very recently, so that you no longer have to send in a second application form to the university as well as your UCAS online application.

The UCAS form

UCAS stands for University and Colleges Admissions Service and it is the central way that you apply to university in the UK. Your UCAS form, when complete, will be emailed to your five chosen universities. They all see exactly the same form so it is important that you do not write anything specific about one university in your Personal Statement, because the other universities may think that you don't want to go there and will not offer you a place.

In September you will have to log on to the UCAS website and register. Go to www.ucas.com/students/apply. In order to do this you will need an email address. If you haven't got one go to yahoo. com or hotmail.com and get a free one. When you register on the UCAS website, you will be sent an application number, user name and password, which you will need every time you log on to UCAS.

The entire application is done online and although it may seem complex and time consuming, you can complete it in stages and come back to it. There is no need to do it all in one sitting. There are help sections all the way through the form in case you get stuck. There are several sections to fill in. Start with your personal details, which include your name, address and date of birth. Then comes student support, which is where you have to select your fee code. If you are a British national your local authority will be your fee payer.

Next is an additional information section in which you can write 'Activities in preparation for higher education'. These activities specifically refer to attending summer schools in preparation for university run by either the universities themselves or trusts such as the Sutton Trust. See www.suttontrust.com/index.asp or contact UCAS for more information (www.ucas.com/about_us/contact_us).

Now we get on to the nitty gritty of the form – the university choices. You can apply to either Oxford or Cambridge. Choose the correct university code from the drop-down menu (CAM C05 for Cambridge and OXF 033 for Oxford). You also need to write what UCAS calls the 'campus code', which is the college code. A drop-down list will appear again. You will also need to choose the subject and select which year of entry you are applying for (i.e. do you intend to take a gap year?).

The next section is very important – education. You need to write down every GCSE and A level (or equivalent qualification) and grade you have taken under the heading of the school in which you took them. If you are applying post-A level you need to write down all of your modules grades. It would be helpful to amass all your GCSE and A level module certificates before you begin this section of the application form to aid the efficient completion of this section.

The next section is employment. This is not the same as work experience although both paid employment and work experience can be discussed in your Personal Statement. This is about jobs you have been paid to do. It doesn't matter how insignificant it sounds to you – write it down. Admissions tutors will be pleased to see that you have had the commitment and maturity to hold down a job, even if it's a paper round.

Next is the Personal Statement – your chance to show the admissions tutors how you write and how informed you are about your subject. You should write this in a Word document, spell check it and read it through carefully and when it is ready, copy and paste it into the UCAS form. The Personal Statement is discussed in more detail in Chapter 5.

The next stage is to send the form off (it goes to your teacher). In order to do this, you have to pay £19 (for the 2009/10 cycle; £9 if you are applying to just one university) to UCAS for processing by credit card (your school may have a policy of paying this for you so you need to check before you part with any money). Your teacher will then be able to open it on the teachers' part of the UCAS site. They will read it to check everything is correct and will then write their reference and predicted grades. Then they will send it off and the universities will receive it immediately.

For Oxford and Cambridge all of this has to happen by 15 October. Your teacher may need some time to write the reference, so do make sure you have your part done well in advance.

Cambridge Supplementary Application Questionnaire

However, that is not quite all. Shortly after your application is received, Cambridge will require a Supplementary Application Questionnaire (SAQ) to be filled out. The SAQ is filled out online and will cost nothing to send. Cambridge requires this so that the university has consistent information about all applicants in order to make fully informed decisions. You will be emailed once your UCAS application form has been received and the email will direct you to a website where you can log on and complete the questionnaire. If you do not have access to email or cannot complete the online form for some other reason, you can contact the Cambridge Admissions Office for a paper version. The initial email will give you a deadline by which you need to have completed the form and this is usually around the end of October. The SAQ has eight sections, which are given below.

1| Photograph – you will need a passport-style colour photograph of yourself, preferably in digital format, which can then be uploaded onto the form.
2| Application type – this section asks very general questions about your application, such as whether you have applied for an Organ Scholarship, if you are taking a gap year or are going through the Special Access Scheme.
3| Personal details – this covers information about you and your own situation, such as where you live, what your first name is, etc.
4| Course details – here, you will be asked to provide information regarding any options available within the course for which you are applying. So, if you are applying to read modern and medieval languages, this section will require you to state which languages you wish to study.
5| Education – in this section, you will be asked about your school(s), such as class sizes and extra help received.
6| Qualifications – in this section, you need to give details, if applicable, of your AS and A level modules, or their equivalents, and the marks you have achieved so far.
7| Additional information – this is where you can add an additional Personal Statement if you would like to. It also asks about your career plans and how you have shown your interest in the subject for which you have applied.
8| Submit – once you have clicked on the submit button, you can't change your answers, so click with care!

The additional statement

Don't panic about this. It's a great opportunity for you to tell the Admissions Tutor just how excited you are about the course and perhaps the college for which you are applying. Unless your Personal Statement on the UCAS application has covered your academic interests absolutely fully, do take advantage of the additional statement to really stand out and show your real understanding of the course. Remember, however, not to duplicate anything you have said on the UCAS form.

You may, for instance, wish to draw attention to specifics in the course content which have attracted you to it over and above the same course at other institutions. The key advantage of mentioning areas of special academic interest (and that includes your wider reading) is that it gives you a chance of getting a predictable question at interview which allows you to shine. Do note though that this section on the form is not an appropriate forum to discuss your childhood dreams of the spires of Oxford or to tell the Admissions Tutor that your main reason for applying is the excellent reputation of Cambridge. Neither of these, of themselves, is sufficient reason for applying and frankly they've been heard before. It's taken for granted that you know of the reputation of both Oxford and Cambridge and the tutor wants facts, not dreams! Here is a good example written by student for his economics application.

I am particularly interested in studying economics at Cambridge as the faculty stresses its commitment to public policy, and I share the view of its importance to the functioning of our daily lives. The course is particularly suited to my interests as I would have the opportunity to specialise in some areas, such as development economics and I would enjoy the academic rigour of applying maths to the analysis of economics. Furthermore, I would be able to draw from my other interests such as politics and history to augment my study of economics. I have started to use SPSS software in order to enhance my theoretical backbone of econometrics and because I enjoy using quantitative methods.

I find the collegiate nature of the university attractive because I cannot get enough of talking about the subject, and nothing is as enjoyable as to share one's interest with others who feel the same way about it! Also, as someone who values perspective, I think that discussing issues with people from different disciplines would facilitate the exchange of ideas and present new angles from which to address points of interest. I am also excited at the opportunity to discuss ideas in supervisions with people who are at the forefront of their field and who are engaged in active research.

Here is one written by a modern languages applicant.

> Having been uncertain at the age of 16 which subjects to con-
> tinue, I am now looking forward with confidence and enthusiasm
> to the challenge of completing French A level in the coming year
> before embarking on a modern languages degree course. The
> emphasis that the modern languages course places on literature
> mirrors my own enthusiasm for French and Italian literature, and I
> was particularly thrilled to note that several lecturers have exper-
> tise in the works of Primo Levi, for whom I have great admiration
> and would love to study at a higher level. As I am thinking of
> becoming a teacher, the idea of the year abroad greatly appeals,
> as it would give me valuable experience of teaching, whilst improv-
> ing my linguistic fluency to a high level.

Oxford additional form

Oxford no longer requires you to complete a second application,
with the three exceptions of: candidates for choral or organ awards,
candidates wishing to be interviewed overseas and graduate applicants for the Accelerated Medical Course.

Some of the information which the Cambridge SAQ requires is
collected in Oxford's case from the government's public information
service. The information which the university will look at is as follows:

- the performance of your school or college at GCSE and A level
  or their equivalents (both using DCSF or equivalent data – in
  both instances a candidate will be flagged if their educational
  establishment performs below the national average)
- the postcode that you live at (assessed using Acorn information –
  where a candidate's postcode falls into groups four or five the
  application will be flagged)
- whether you have been looked after/in care for more than three
  months (determined from the UCAS application)
- whether you have participated in either a Sutton Trust summer
  school or the Oxford Young Ambassador Scheme.

If you are applying for law or medicine at either university you have to
apply online well before 15 October to take a special exam called the
LNAT (for Law) or the BMAT (for Medicine). You will be emailed a
LNAT/BMAT reference number and you need to enter this reference
number on your UCAS form. This and the other written exams are
the subject of the next chapter. In addition, you may need to send
some written work. There is a separate cover sheet for this and your

school should give it to you. You can also download it from the admissions website. As usual, if in doubt, call the admissions office.

Written work to be submitted

Once you have completed your application form(s), you need to consider submitting written work. If you have applied to Oxford, you will need to submit marked work where you have applied for the following subjects:

- archaeology and anthropology
- classical archaeology and ancient history
- classics
- classics and English
- classics and modern languages
- classics and oriental studies
- computer science
- economics and management
- English language and literature
- English and modern languages
- European and Middle Eastern languages
- experimental psychology
- fine art
- geography
- history
- history (ancient and modern)
- history and economics
- history and English
- history and modern languages
- history and politics
- history of art
- law (jurisprudence) and law with law studies in Europe
- mathematics
- mathematics and computer science
- mathematics and philosophy
- mathematics and statistics
- medicine
- modern languages
- modern languages and linguistics
- music
- oriental studies
- philosophy and modern languages
- philosophy and theology
- PPE
- physics
- physics and philosophy

- physiological sciences
- PPP
- theology.

The Oxford prospectus gives clear instructions as to what you need to send and by when. Remember to inform your teachers in advance that you will need to send marked work.

At Cambridge, each college has a different policy on written work, but you are more likely to be asked to send in work where you have applied to read an arts or social science subject. The college will contact you directly if they require work from you.

The submitted essay is often used as the starting point for discussion in the interview. The essay can show us whether the candidate has the ability to argue and has academic confidence. One student submitted an essay that his teacher marked as a grade B minus, but he was confident of his work and we valued his confidence.

Admissions Tutor, Cambridge

What qualities are Oxford and Cambridge looking for?

Let us step back and consider the qualities for which Oxford and Cambridge are looking.

They want to know that you:

- have an ability and readiness to join in discussion of the subject
- have an understanding and commitment to the subject
- know major developments in the subject
- know why you want to study it
- know what the course at Oxford or Cambridge entails and that you are suited to it.

We look for whether the candidates show stamina, independence, ambition, commitment and organisational skills in order to assess whether they can survive the intense and pressured atmosphere that is Cambridge.

Admissions Tutor, Cambridge

A successful applicant will be:

- *well-informed and very keen to learn more*
- *not satisfied with the status quo of their knowledge*
- *determined to get to the bottom of any question put in front of them*

57

■ *must be a pleasure to teach on a one-to-one basis a couple of hours a week*

■ *will make the most contribution to the college in academic terms.*

Admissions Tutor, Cambridge

How can you demonstrate these things and in which document (reference, Personal Statement, 'extra Personal Statement', submitted work or interview) do you think they will appear?

Have an ability and readiness to join in discussion of the subject

Your subject teachers will make a comment to the teacher who writes the reference as to how much you participate in class. Make sure you start doing this. Your reference should contain evidence of this quality.

Have an understanding and commitment to the subject

You need to have read around your subject – ask your teacher for a book list or go to the faculty website for Oxford or Cambridge for your subject, download the first-year reading list and pick a few books. If in doubt, speak to the admissions tutor directly.

You need to demonstrate a sustained commitment to your subject. Can you prove that your interest in your subject has been growing over a long time? Have you gone to conferences and lectures? Your Personal Statement should contain evidence of this quality.

Know major developments in the subject

You need to keep abreast of current affairs in your field and in general. Start keeping a current affairs diary. Each day go to the BBC news website (http://news.bbc.co.uk) or read a quality newspaper (*Telegraph, Independent, The Times,* etc.) and write down five headlines in your diary. To keep abreast of current affairs in your field you can click on the type of news, for example, science or health on the BBC news website. There are also specialist journals you should be reading regularly such as *New Scientist* or *The Economist*. Ask your teacher to recommend some journals. Subject-specific headlines also need to be noted in your diary. Before your interview you should re-read your current affairs diary.

Know why you want to study it

You will most certainly be asked this at interview and you need to explain the reasons clearly in your Personal Statement. Just like with your A level choice, you need to make sure that your choice of course sounds informed and planned. Be prepared to tell the story as to how you became interested in the subject and what you may intend to do with it.

Know what the course at Oxford or Cambridge entails and that you are suited to it

You need to have read the course description thoroughly and be able to explain what you will study in each year. The course web-pages will explain this in depth. The course at Oxford or Cambridge is often very different from that at other universities. Clearly, your UCAS Personal Statement is not the place to extol the virtues of Oxford and Cambridge as the other universities will see it too. The place to demonstrate that you know what the course entails is the 'extra Personal Statement' and in your interview.

Checklist

- The UCAS form is completed online (£19/£9).
- There are no extra paper forms to complete.
- Cambridge will email you with a link to a Supplementary Application Questionnaire.
- You need to check the Oxford prospectus to see if you need to send in written work.
- Get all your GCSE and A level module certificates together so that you can quickly write down all the information.
- Keep a current affairs diary.
- Get hold of the reading lists from the first-year courses.
- Ask your teachers to recommend extra reading.
- Keep a log book of the lectures and other events you attend.

05

The Personal Statement

According to Cambridge, each applicant is assessed on six criteria to give a holistic view of the student:

1| academic record (GCSE and AS)
2| school/college reference
3| Personal Statement
4| submitted work where requested
5| test results
6| performance at interview.

(Source: Applying to Cambridge: Advice for teachers, Tutors and HE Advisers 2008 Entry.)

There's not a great deal you can now do about the GCSE and AS results you already have, but you can now impress the admissions tutors in around 47 lines of information about how fantastic you are in your Personal Statement. This is your chance. You need to prepare your Personal Statement carefully and be prepared for the fact that you may have to discuss it at interview. Not all tutors will ask you about it but some may, so it's vital not to write about anything you cannot discuss. For example, if you mention a book you enjoyed reading about your subject make sure you reread it and can talk about it in detail. You need to be able to substantiate everything you say in your Personal Statement.

The Personal Statement is most likely to be the most difficult document a 17-year-old will have written – there are many complexities such as how to fine-tune the tone of the statement so that it is not too boastful but able to sell the student.

Admissions Tutor, Cambridge

The first point to make is that the Personal Statement should be personal. That means – don't copy from someone else or from a website. There are cases of students using very old Personal Statements from friends who have applied years before. Be careful if you are tempted to do this because UCAS now has a system called the 'Similarity Detection Service', which can detect if certain word combinations have been used before. If the computer finds a very close match then a letter is sent to all of your university choices and they are told that your statement has been copied from a previous applicant. At that point it is up to the universities to decide how to deal with the fraudulent student. It is fraud, by the way, as in the last part of the UCAS form you have to declare that everything on the form is true. Clearly Oxford or Cambridge will not bother to look at a candidate if it comes to their attention that the potential student has plagiarised somebody else's work. So even though you may be deeply impressed by the phrasing used by someone else in their Personal Statement, don't copy it. The best thing to do if you see something you like the sound of is to think about what message it is getting across. Then ask yourself whether that is the same message you need to deliver too. If so, think about how you would say this to a friend. Then you are on the way to putting it into your own words.

What should go into a Personal Statement?

The subject-related content of the Personal Statement ought to take priority. An admissions tutor will read the Personal Statement asking themselves the following questions about the candidate.

- *Have they chosen the right subject for the right reasons?*
- *Can they survive in an intense and pressured atmosphere?*
- *Do they have a range of interests and aptitudes?*
- *Does the Personal Statement confirm their depth of interest in the subject?*
- *What has the candidate studied independently?*

Admissions Tutor, Cambridge

Perhaps the best way of answering this question is to consider the purpose of the Personal Statement. The first thing that Oxford and Cambridge will look at is whether you have been predicted three As. Let's assume you have. They may also want to see at least six glittering A*s at GCSE and a glowing reference from your teacher. It used to be the case that almost all applicants to Oxford and Cambridge got an interview and at that stage the best were differentiated from the second best. However, due to the sheer volume of applicants these days, Oxford and Cambridge cannot invite all applicants to interview.

All things being equal, with two (or more) candidates having the same calibre of reference and the same examination grades, they will next turn to the Personal Statement to try to differentiate students. After selecting a certain number of candidates to interview, depending on the subject they may ask the applicant to sit an exam before the interview. For some very oversubscribed subjects you can get 'deselected' (rejected) at this stage. You can also be deselected if your module scores are not high enough for some subjects. For example, if you have not got 90% in most of your maths modules and you are applying for engineering you may well be deselected. Finally, you will be called to interview. The Personal Statement is also the place where you can explain what you intend to do in your gap year if applicable.

Overall, remember that the Personal Statement is a sales pitch! You are selling yourself as a potentially excellent undergraduate. So what makes an excellent undergraduate? The basics are: someone who is committed to their subject, with a track record of showing that interest, someone who is hard working and able to stick at the course for its duration. You can show these in the following ways.

Commitment to and interest in your subject

This can be shown by your extra-curricular reading and attendance at any lectures. This will also be proven through work experience. Have a look at Chapter 3 (Preparing to apply) for some help on this.

Hard working and able to stick at the course

You will show the admissions officer your ability to work hard mainly through your examination results so far, but this, and your ability to stay for the duration, will also be evidenced by any work experience you have done, or projects you have been involved in such as the Duke of Edinburgh's Award Scheme. Your gap year plans will also show this if they are appropriate.

Admissions officers are interested in your extra-curricular activities, but do remember that this is an academic application, so your interest in the subject is far more important than your captaining the hockey team. Do mention them, but I wouldn't recommend that you spend any more than a third of the document on them. The majority needs to cover the questions which were looked at in Chapter 3. Tell them how you became interested in your subject. Let's take the example of Spanish and Portuguese, which is what I applied to read at Cambridge. My own interest was piqued by an inspirational teacher, who not only taught me the language and literature of Spain, but also showed me how to cook Spanish food and took my class to see Spanish and South American films. Her passion was utterly infectious, so that year on year, I was inspired to learn more and more. I visited Spain every holiday and went to live there with a Spanish family for eight weeks one summer holiday. I went to exhibitions of Spanish artists and cooked every Spanish dish

I was able to. We studied a specific number of texts at A level and I ensured that I read other books by those same authors. Because Portuguese was to be a new language for me at Cambridge, I arranged to spend a month in Lisbon on a month-long language course for beginners during the summer before I applied. I mentioned all of this in my Personal Statement before I even touched upon the hockey team!

The Personal Statement will have to contain something that makes the interviewer want to meet you. You have to sound interesting and show that you are serious about studying your subject. Here we can have a look at a section of a previous student's Personal Statement. (Students have kindly allowed us to publish their Personal Statements here but do be careful not to copy any of them.)

> *Applicants who are not invited for interview are unsuccessful because their academic track record, admission test performance (where appropriate) and school/college reference indicate that they have no realistic chance of winning a place, not because their Personal Statement let them down.*
> **Director of Admissions, Cambridge Colleges**

How long should a Personal Statement be?

There isn't a specific word limit as such but this section of the UCAS form does have a space limit (47 lines) and a limit of 4,000 characters. Forty-eight lines, as a rough guide, corresponds to about 700 words but it depends on how you divide up your paragraphs and whether you leave a line between paragraphs (it is up to you if you do this). I would advise you to write your draft Personal Statement on a computer and after you have revisited it several times you can copy and paste it into the online UCAS form. For details about how to navigate your way through the UCAS form go to www.ucas.com.

Adam's Personal Statement

Adam applied to Cambridge to read economics. He was asked for an interview.

Paragraph 1

Physics answers the question of why. Maths is a tool to solve quantitative issues. Politics is the study of the structure of law, government and policy. Economics, as I see it, is everything in between.

The introduction needs to capture the Admissions Tutor's attention and make them want to read on. I think this introduction is punchy. It doesn't say that he doesn't enjoy the study of his other A levels but it explains why he thinks economics is so good.

Paragraph 2

> I thoroughly enjoy and am extremely interested in Economics. I believe that the distinct view on the world that economists have and the power to do good is why I am so enthused about the subject. I'm particularly drawn to Development Economics, but acknowledge the role that other spheres of Economics such as Econometrics, Micro and Macroeconomics play in the constitution of this field. This is why my current goal as a student of Economics is to learn as much about the subject in general. To this end, I have read several works of prominent economists. Delving into mind-expanding texts such as 'Development as Freedom', 'Capitalism and Freedom', 'Globalisation and its Discontents' and 'Wealth of Nations'. In addition to my individual exploration, I have attended courses at Harvard University and at Brown University for Economics and Global Development respectively.

This paragraph has the effect of making me believe that Adam has a serious interest in economics. He has identified a field of economics that he is particularly drawn to. The danger of making such a comment is that he is giving the admissions tutor ammunition – the admissions tutor may ask him detailed questions about his understanding of development economics. This is not a bad thing; it just means he needs to be prepared to answer questions about this topic. Adam mentions several well-known books about economics. However, he has not given the authors' names, which in my view is a mistake even though some of the books are very well known. I would have preferred to have seen 'Adam Smith's *Wealth of Nations*' or '*Wealth of Nations* by Adam Smith'. This is because at university, referencing works correctly becomes increasingly important. Attending university courses in a summer, or going to some sort of master class is an excellent way to show that you are really interested in studying the subject.

Paragraph 3

My passion for Economics, especially Development Economics, comes as a result of my background and experiences. I have been fortunate enough to travel, experience different cultures, lifestyles and perspectives. Seeing suffering and poverty, through community service and observation, has made me internalise these issues. Possessing a heritage that combines both economically developed and developing nations as I have lived in both Costa Rica and Britain has underlined this problem for me. Throughout my life, I have seen myself as a problem solver and I believe this has been highlighted through Young Enterprise. Being Head of Production, I was in charge of overcoming difficulties such as rising costs. We did not win in the end, but it was a great learning experience and one that showed me the importance of thinking creatively.

This paragraph cleverly manages to relay the fact that Adam has had an interesting life as he has lived in two very different countries and reinforces the fact that he is really interested in economics. It also explains that he took part in extra-curricular activities at school, which shows that he was not only able to handle his A level workload, but could take on extra responsibility. Being involved in Young Enterprise also demonstrates that Adam can work as a member of a team, which is an important quality that an admissions tutor may appreciate. (Young Enterprise is a national competition where you can set up a business in a team when you are in Year 12 in order to gain experience of marketing, financial modelling and strategy. You are assessed on different facets of business and can win a prize for excellence in these fields and overall. Ask your teacher for more information.)

Paragraph 4

I was selected to attend a Presidential Classroom programme in Washington DC and with great enthusiasm was able to debate and learn more in depth about the functioning of government and policy. I was also selected to represent my school in the University of Costa Rica's Law competition for schools which we won. That taught me the importance of different points of view and acknowledging them. Having to argue either for a multinational corporation to construct an energy plant or for the preservation of the environment and the interests of the town affected by the construction.

This paragraph clearly shows that Adam has taken part in extra-curricular activities. More than just list them, Adam has explained what he got out of them, which shows that he thinks about his own development carefully.

Paragraph 5

Aside from travelling and learning, I appreciate the Arts and sports greatly. Acting is a passion of mine and started by attending Theatre Saturday School at the age of six. Since then I have been involved in different types of work, for instance, I was involved with a professional children's production which produced the play 'Annie' and I played the lead male role. In the arena of sports, I am a keen footballer. I played for the 1st XI football team at my school.

Most students put in a short paragraph detailing other extra-curricular activities that do not relate to their academic subject. This helps give the impression that you are an all-rounder. This type of paragraph is less important than the others but at least a couple of lines should be there.

Closing sentence

Economics has developed into my newest and greatest interest as it seems to combine not only all my academic endeavours but also permeates my pursuits out of the classroom.

It is not necessary to have a closing sentence and sometimes they can sound a bit false. If you do feel a need to sum up, then Adam's sentence is a good example.

Now have a go writing your first draft. You are going to be editing your draft many times and showing it to many people, so it will not be perfect by any means. The way to write the best Personal Statement is to give yourself several weeks – maybe eight. I advise my students to write their first draft in their third term of their AS year. If you leave it for a couple of weeks and then come back to it, you will be sufficiently removed from it that you will be able to critically analyse your own work.

You need to get various people to read your draft of your Personal Statement. Ask your friends and family to read it and give them a pen so that they can read actively. Ask them if your Personal Statement gives a flavour of you, not only in terms of content but also in terms of writing style. It is very important that there are no spelling or grammatical mistakes as these stand out like a sore thumb and create a bad impression. Hopefully your friends and family will be able to spot these. When you have made or considered making the changes they suggest, give the Personal Statement to your teacher to read for their comments. Remember, you do not have to take everyone's comments on board, if you disagree with something then trust your own judgement. Your writing style will say as much to the admissions tutor as the content. After all, for every course at Oxford or Cambridge you will have to express your ideas very well in weekly essays.

We are now going to read part of another applicant's Personal Statement that details her work experience. Helena applied to read medicine at Cambridge and was invited for interview.

▓ Excerpt from Helena's Personal Statement

I organised some work experience in the orthopaedic wing of Nottingham Hospital and at my local GP clinic. At Nottingham Hospital, I shadowed the doctors on their ward round, watched a number of knee replacements and observed fracture clinic which made me realise how such a simple procedure can dramatically increase the quality of life in older people. This is such a stark contrast with my experiences in Uganda where living to 70 is seen as something of a miracle. A further thing I learnt from my work experience is the importance of patient–doctor relationships, and this is one of the factors which really draws me to Medicine. I saw this most particularly in my work experience with a GP where I saw him take on a central role of trust within the community.

I have had much opportunity to develop my interpersonal skills. During my Sixth Form I worked with underprivileged children at an after-school club in London. I have volunteered in a charity shop and this year I am volunteering one day a week at St Peter's Hospice in Green Town. I am able to easily relate to people and enjoy meeting, getting to know and trying to help different people. I used this skill when I was deputy head girl of my school, where I was involved in talking to students and helping them with any problems they might have. I keep up to date with the news, reading about medical developments in the 'BMJ' and the 'New Scientist'.

Helena has clearly gone to a great deal of trouble to organise work experience. She has woven her experiences into her narrative about why she wants to do medicine and why she thinks she would be good at it.

Imogen's Personal Statement

Finally, we are going to read another Personal Statement in its entirety. Imogen applied to Oxford to read French and Italian. She was invited to interview.

In a world where increasing numbers of people speak English, it may seem superfluous for students to put their efforts into acquiring foreign languages. For me, however, language is not just a means by which we communicate, but the barrier of language often hides whole worlds of literature and culture which can remain inaccessible, even through translation. For this reason, language as a whole is a source of fascination for me, resulting in a desire to focus on Italian, which I did at A level, and French, a language I very much enjoyed at GCSE and which I feel complements Italian well. I have therefore resolved to take a one year French A level course during my gap year, enabling me to study it at university.

I think literature portrays language at its best, as it is the means by which a language displays the full range of its versatility and the essence of the people who communicate through it. It often offers a window into the culture it describes, which I feel is especially well achieved by Natalia Ginzburg. After studying 'Le Voci della Sera' at A level, I read 'La Strada che Va in Citta' and 'E Stato Cosi', finding that her depiction of the various female characters strongly impresses upon the reader the difficulties faced by these women in the light of their religion and community. One sympathises easily with them as they struggle to find happiness, owing largely to Ginzburg's simple and often stark narrative. Similarly, I admire Primo Levi for the style in which he narrates, maintaining a dignified approach to the experiences he describes. In 'Se Non Ora, Quando?' his depiction of Italy is striking: an oasis of freedom, where Jews and Christians are indistinguishable.

To help improve my French I have read various works of literature and philosophy. Interested in the problem of evil through Philosophy A level, I read Voltaire's 'Zadig', which demonstrates how suffering is unavoidable, but that sense and perseverance will see a man through. This, however, does little to solve the theological problem of evil. Nor does Candide twelve years later, but it highlights flaws in the ideology that 'tout est au mieux', or 'all is for the best', and points forward to suggest how to live happily in spite of evil. I subscribe to the literary magazine 'Virgule', through which I discovered Pierre de Ronsard, in whom I was delighted to find traces of Petrarch, by whom I have read some Canzoniere, and numerous classical authors that I have studied. I read a selection of Les Amours, and found that there was much opportunity for intertextual comparison with the texts I have studied in the past.

Last summer I worked as an au pair in France, which improved my French enormously, not only giving me an understanding of French daily life, but also valuable experience of the world of work. At school I was awarded the Prize for Classics and Italian, for linguistic success and contribution to these areas. Outside academic concerns, I was a Managing Director of a Young Enterprise company in Year 12, and have completed the Silver Duke of Edinburgh award, as well as a qualification in youth leadership, which I hope have made me responsible and motivated. In addition to playing the piano, I sang in two choirs at school and continue to take lessons, focusing on Italian arias. Alongside my studies this year, I follow Italian current affairs by transcribing the TG2 news, and am taking conversation classes weekly. I am also taking classes at the Institut Français in London to help me become more fluent in French, and shall continue to read avidly, exploring as many authors as possible.

Imogen comes across as a diligent and highly interested student. She is widely read and seems to be an interesting person. Would you interview her? In summary, make sure that you emphasise your academic side, be very specific about your experiences and interests and of course, be personal!

▓ Checklist

- ▪ Start working on your Personal Statement many months before the application is due in.

06 International students

English language requirements

It is essential that your English language skills are good enough for you to cope with the intensive nature of the courses, all of which are taught and examined in English. If your first language is not English, one of the following formal qualifications is required by the universities:

- GCSE in English Language/IGCSE English Language/O Level (as a first language): at grade C or above for Cambridge or grade B for Oxford
- IELTS: normally a minimum overall grade of 7.0, usually with 7.0 in each element
- TOEFL: an overall score of 100 on the internet-based test
- for EU students, a high grade in English taken as part of a leaving examination (e.g. the European Baccalaureate, the French Baccalaureate, Abitur, etc.) may be acceptable
- Cambridge Certificate in Advanced English: at grade A
- Cambridge Certificate of Proficiency in English: at grade A or B.

Qualifications

Both universities will accept non-UK qualifications, of course, but they will, as with A levels, need to be passed at the very highest level. Cambridge asks that you contact the university as soon as possible to discuss the qualifications you will be gaining, whereas for Oxford see the website at www.admissions.ox.ac.uk/int/quals.shtml.

Applying

Cambridge

You will need to complete an electronic UCAS application in the same way as a home student and you will also have to complete a Cambridge Overseas Application Form (COAF), which is available from the Cambridge Admissions Office. Once you have filled it in, you must ensure that it is returned to them by 15 October, which is the same deadline as the UCAS form.

Cambridge conducts interviews for some overseas applicants in their home country. In the past the university has interviewed in Hong Kong, Malaysia, Singapore and China. To find out if the university will be interviewing in your country, or in a country close to you, you will have to check the website in the summer before you apply. If you choose to do this, your COAF must reach the university by 20 September.

Oxford

You can download the application material for Oxford from www.admissions.ox.ac.uk/forms and you will need to return the forms by the usual deadline of 15 October. If, however, you want to be interviewed at one of Oxford's international centres (North America, India, Hong Kong, Singapore and Malaysia), you will have to have your application in by 20 September. If you are unable to attend one of the centres, the college to which you have applied may be able to interview you over the telephone. All interviews for medicine and fine art take place at Oxford though, so if you are applying to read one of these subjects, you must make arrangements to travel to the UK.

Finances

As has already been mentioned, fees for non-EU students are significantly higher than for home students. At both universities, you will need to provide evidence of your ability to fund your entire course. Remember that you will have to take into account your living expenses as well as the tuition fees. Neither university will allow you to take paid employment while you are there, so you won't be able to rely on getting a job to pay your way! For living expenses, you should probably allow around £7,500, but this will depend on the style in which you live. Remember also that if you have nowhere to live in the holidays, you will have to allow for higher expenses.

Financial support and scholarships

Neither university offers a great many scholarships for overseas students, but each college has some funding for international students. Full details can be found online.

07 Written tests

For some subjects, you may have to take a test when you get to Oxford or Cambridge, before your interview, or you may have to take an exam in your own school well before the interview. See Tables 4 and 5 below for a list. Oxford has a very standardised approach whereas Cambridge has a more ad hoc policy on exams that varies from college to college.

> *Tests such as BMAT, LNAT and HAT are crucial in deciding who is interviewed.*
>
> **Admissions Tutor, Oxford**

The processes are different at Oxford and Cambridge although there are some similarities. The bottom line is that tutors want to choose students who will get the best grades in their final year. But how do you know who these students are? All the students applying have or are predicted to get all As at A level. Also A level often tests factual recall, but what other skills are needed at university?

The answer is that being able to read a passage and understand what can and can't be surmised by that passage is one of the things that is important – in other words, critical analysis. Not only is this a useful skill at university when conducting research for your essays but also it is important in life in general. In fact, the top employers, for example, civil service fast stream and investment banks, have been testing these skills for years in very similar tests.

Applying to Oxford

The first thing you have to do is read the prospectus or go to the Oxford admissions website to find out if your subject requires tests. If your subject does require a test, download the sample tests from www.admissions.ox.ac.uk/interviews/tests. The test you sit will be the same at every college. It may or may not be referred to in your interview.

Applying to Cambridge

At Cambridge, for most subjects there is no centralised system. Different colleges set different written exams at interview for the

Table 4: Subjects in which tests form part of the entry requirements at Oxford

Subject	Test
Economics and management	TSA
English	ELAT
History	HAT
Law	LNAT
Maths Maths with computer science, philosophy or statistics Computer sciences	Aptitude test for maths and computer science
Medicine and physiological sciences	BMAT
Physics	Physics Aptitude Test
Physics and philosophy	Physics Aptitude Test
PPP	Under review
Experimental psychology	Under review
PPE	TSA

same course and different colleges may or may not set exams even for the same subject. The way to look it up is to go to www.cam.ac.uk/admissions/undergraduate/courses. You need to click on your selected course. On the right-hand side of the next screen is a box entitled 'At a glance'. The fourth hyperlink down says 'Admissions test' – click on the link. A new page will come up with a list of all the colleges and the requirements for your subject. If we take the engineering page as an example (www.cam.ac.uk/admissions/undergraduate/courses/engineering/tests.html) we can see that at some colleges they use the TSA, at others they use an interview only, at some they use their own test at interview and at others they use both their own test at interview and the TSA.

Apart from the subjects that require you to sit tests at interview, there are others that require you to sit a test well before your interview. See Table 5.

BMAT and the maths and physics tests require specialist knowledge and facts need to be revised.

▨ BMAT (BioMedical Admissions Test)

For applications to medicine (Oxford and Cambridge), physiological sciences (Oxford) and veterinary science (Cambridge).

Table 5: Subjects in which tests form part of the entry requirements at Cambridge

Subject	Test
Computer science, economics, engineering, land economy, natural sciences (physical and biological) and social and political sciences	TSA (used by some colleges)
Maths	STEP (used by almost all colleges)
Medicine and veterinary medicine	BMAT

Some universities, including Oxford and Cambridge, require students applying for medical school and for veterinary science to sit the BMAT exam. It is clear is that the BMAT is very important in deciding whether or not you will be accepted at Oxford and Cambridge. It aims to provide a predictive assessment of your potential for a medical degree. As such it is a demanding test.

Let us look more closely at BMAT and what it entails. You need to apply online to register for BMAT. It is a two-hour paper that is sat at your school. There are three sections:

1| aptitude and skills (60 minutes, multiple choice)
2| scientific knowledge and applications (30 minutes, multiple choice)
3| essay writing task (30 minutes).

You have to pay a fee for BMAT (the standard fee is £32.10), which can be waived if you are in receipt of full EMA (education maintenance allowance). Go to www.bmat.org.uk/faqstudent.html#gen15 for more information. Use a pencil for the multiple choice sections and a ballpoint pen for the essay question. Answer all questions – you are not penalised for wrong answers. You will have to find out the date by which you must register for BMAT but it is likely to be by the end of September, or by mid-October if you pay a late entry penalty. The BMAT exam usually takes place at the beginning of November.

What do you need to revise for BMAT?

BMAT requires GCSE-level knowledge of maths and GCSE Dual Science Award knowledge of biology, chemistry and physics. This does not mean hazily remembering your GCSE days. This means active revision. For many medics, physics and maths may be a thing of the past – but you have to revise them thoroughly for the exam.

75

The exam is structured such that biology, chemistry and physics are equally weighted and maths is slightly less. Go through your old exam questions, or buy a GCSE revision guide. If you have not written an essay for two years it is worth practising and perhaps showing to your old English or history teacher. Here are two essay titles that are similar to the 2007 BMAT essay questions:

- Is longevity shaking the foundations of society and changing attitudes to life and death?
- The technology of medicine will outrun society. Discuss.

How Oxford and Cambridge use the BMAT score

Oxford and Cambridge will look at the scores of each section individually. Cambridge tutors believe that Sections 1 and 2 correlate best with Tripos performance and therefore put an emphasis on doing well in those sections. Although the first section cannot be revised for, the second section can be heavily revised for. Unfortunately for those people who write well, even if you get a very high mark for the essay, the most important thing Cambridge cares about is Sections 1 and 2. Oxford will deselect medical applicants on the basis of their GCSEs and BMAT score. This means that if these grades are low, you will not be invited to interview.

BMAT example questions

Section 1 question 2

2 'The UK government wishes to increase the number of young people from poorer families entering university education. However, it has recently changed the way in which it provides financial support for students. Whereas it used to provide grants that the student did not need to repay, it now provides loans that the student must repay when he or she enters employment. Research shows that students from poorer families are more likely to be deterred from going to university by the prospect of debt.'

Which one of the following is an inference that can be drawn from the passage above?

A Students from poorer families are less interested in entering university.
B Universities will not be willing to help meet the government's target.
C The government's action is likely to deter poorer students from going to university more than richer.

D   The prospect of debt is a deterrent to all students, not just the poorer ones.

E   Maintenance grants were too expensive for the government to fund.

Section 3 - Writing task (30 minutes)

Our genes evolved for a Stone Age life style. Therefore, we must adopt Stone Age habits if we are to be healthy.

Write a unified essay in which you address the following.

■   Explain the logical connexion between the two sentences.
■   What might be the practical implications If we were to agree with the reasoning?
■   Discuss the extent to which the argument is valid.

Source: From the specimen papers available on the Cambridge Assessment website (www.admissionstests.cambridgeassessment.org.uk). Reprinted by permission of the University of Cambridge Local Examinations Syndicate.

ELAT (English Literature Aptitude Test)

For applications to English at Oxford only.

The ELAT tests applicants' ability in the close reading of an unfamiliar text and the construction of a focused essay. Like the BMAT, the ELAT takes place at your school, so you must ask it to register you for the test. You need to find out the date by which you need to apply. The exam takes place in late October or early November. It lasts for 90 minutes and is free of charge. You will be given six poems or prose passages and will be asked compare and contrast two or three of them in a way that seems interesting to you. All six passages will be linked in some way and this will be made clear to you. It is very important to look at the sample paper and go through the mark scheme. For more information go to www.elat.org.uk. Your score will be placed into one of four bands, and those whose scores lie the top two bands are the most likely to be called for interview.

Look at the box for a sample question from the ELAT test. For copyright reasons, we are unable to reproduce the extracts to which the questions refer. This means that you will not be able to try to answer the questions, but we felt it was still worthwhile giving the example questions in order to give a flavour of the style of the test

ELAT sample questions

The following poems and extracts from longer texts present views of fathers, mainly as seen by their children. Read all the material carefully, and then complete the task below.

(a) An extract from a novel by Philip Roth, *The Human Stain*, published in 2001.

(b) 'To the Reverend Shade of His Religious Father', a poem by Robert Herrick (1591–1674).

(c) An extract from a novel by Samuel Richardson, *Clarissa*, 1740, vol. 1, Letter VIII. The novel is written entirely as a sequence of letters.

(d) *Carousel*, a poem by Lucinda Roy; first published in 1988.

(e) *Father's Bedroom*, a poem by Robert Lowell (1917–1977).

(f) An extract from a short story, *Grocer's Daughter*, published in 1987, by Marianne Wiggins.

Task:

Select two or three of the passages (a) to (f) and compare and contrast them in any ways that seem interesting to you, paying particular attention to distinctive features of structure, language and style. In your introduction, indicate briefly what you intend to explore or illustrate through close reading of your chosen passages.

This task is designed to assess your responsiveness to unfamiliar literary material and your skills in close reading. Marks are not awarded for references to other texts or authors you have studied.

Source: From the specimen papers available on the Cambridge Assessment website (www.admissionstests.cambridgeassessment.org.uk). Reprinted by permission of the University of Cambridge Local Examinations Syndicate.

HAT (History Aptitude Test)

For applications to history at Oxford only.

The HAT is testing that you can read critically and write with clarity. You need to revise your history A level syllabus thoroughly as you will be asked to give an example of a situation from the history periods you have studied. The best way to practise HAT is to work through all the past papers and mark schemes, which can be downloaded from www.history.ox.ac.uk/prosundergrad/applying/hat_introduction.htm.

Read one of the sample answers and mark it as if you were the admissions tutor – what do you think are the key points? Then compare your marks with the mark scheme and check that you understand what is being tested. A brief overview will show you that being able to summarise an argument without simply quoting huge chunks is considered to be very important and another point that comes through is how important it is to be focused on your answer.

The HAT is taken at your school and is free. It lasts for two hours and will be sat on a day at the end of October or beginning of November. For an explanation of the structure of the test see www.history. ox.ac.uk/prosundergrad/applying/hat_specification.htm. The test is meant to be of a difficulty similar to the Advanced Extension Award.

The interviewers will look at your score as well as your reference and qualifications to reach a decision about whom to interview. In addition, a homework will need to be submitted (check the faculty website for the submission deadline) and may be used as a basis for discussion at interview. The HAT will not be discussed at interview. Oxford automatically will send the HAT to your school. In general, the people who score in the bottom 20% of HAT will be deselected.

HAT example question

Oxford Colleges History Aptitude Test. October 31st 2007.

Question one (70 marks)

This is an adapted extract from a book about Renaissance Europe. Please read through the extract carefully and think about what it is trying to say. You do not need to know anything about the topic or the period to answer the questions below.

What all governments had in common was a striving to extend effective control over their subjects and to link the most common contemporary meaning of the word 'state' – the power structure, that is, represented by a ruler and his ministers and chief officials – to the significance of what was then a less familiar usage: the state as a geographical catchment area of individuals owing a common obedience to central government. Whatever the terminology employed, the aim was the same: to make a ruler potent and unchallenged within his whole kingdom, to extend effective administration across it, to stimulate shared responses within the commonwealth of compatriots. The aim was hampered by earlier and stubbornly held assumptions about the government's function: to preserve, and if judged appropriate extend, territory that had been won in the past; to protect legally defined privileges while striving to ensure that all men had access to 'good justice'; to tax sparingly, for the common good and with advice; to foster

the rights and influence of 'true religion'. These were conserva-
tive values.

When rulers, whether a king of France or a doge of Venice, swore
to observe them at their coronation or election, they vowed in
effect to stop the historical process in its tracks. Yet in all cases,
governments were forced to alter the status quo by the need to
raise more money. As the tempo of international relations quick-
ened from the later fifteenth century, the costs of diplomacy, from
ambassadors to spies, rose to match their pace. The size of
armies grew: from 12–30,000 before 1500, to 85,000 in the
1570s, to 100,000 and more by the 1620s. Better cannon meant
that fortresses and town walls had to be rebuilt or strengthened.
And war could throw up massive extras: to redeem the sons
Francis I of France had left in Spain after his capture at the battle
of Pavia in 1525 cost the equivalent of 3.6 tons of solid gold. As
all governments were forced throughout the sixteenth century to
spend more on war or defence or both, revenues had to rise: in
France, for example, from 3.5 million livres in 1497 to 15 million
in 1596, in Castile from 850,000 ducats in 1504 to 13 million in
1598. Overall in the course of the century state revenues rose by
a factor of five. This was mainly due to the necessities of war,
partly to voluntary expenditure on buildings and on lavish courts
to inflate the ruler's image. It was also due to larger government
payrolls. However ingenious governments were at postponing
taxes by raising bridging loans from financiers, repayments, like
normal expenditure, had to be met from internal revenues. And
this involved extending the reach of administrative fingers into
pockets previously guarded from them.

To do this, and to ensure the law and order that made administration effective, more officials had to be maintained. At the lowest
level the numbers of copyists and file-clerks and book-keepers
employed by earlier governments became inflated. New tasks,
notably Spain's acquisition of territories in America and Italy,
involved the creation of new governmental committees, but other
governments, too, enlarged the departments which had dealt
with different aspects of business: finance, foreign affairs, legal
issues. Above this proletariat of inky toilers there was a thicken-
ing stratum of supervisors who not only co-ordinated the work of
their departments but offered advice on knotty or debatable
issues. It is at this level of responsibility that their prominence in
contemporary records allows them to be counted: between three
and four times the number shortly after 1600 than around 1500.
In absolute terms this is unimpressive. In mid-sixteenth century

France, for instance, with a population of about 18 million, there were no more than three thousand or so. And there were never enough of them, whether operating at the heart of government or in the provinces, to pump obedience along the venous system that connected a capital with a country as a whole to the extent which new legislation called for.

(a) What are the principal points made by the author in the first paragraph?
    Use your own words and do not write more than 15 lines.
    (10 marks)

(b) Why, in the author's view, did the institutions of government grow in the period under discussion? Write an answer of about one side in length.
    (20 marks)

(c) In an essay of two or three sides, identify and discuss the most important factors that changed the relationship between rulers and ruled in a period with which you are familiar.
    (40 marks)

Source: This question is taken from the HAT paper for 2007. This and all other HAT papers can be accessed at: http://www.history.ox.ac.uk/prosunder-grad/applying/hat_introduction.htm

LNAT (Law National Admissions Test)

For applications to law at Oxford.

Cambridge will ask you to sit their own written test at interview. This will take place for the first time for October 2010 applicants, therefore no sample papers or other information was available at the time of writing.

If you are applying for law at Oxford, and indeed at a handful of other universities, you will need to sit LNAT.

LNAT is a two-hour test. There are two parts, a multiple choice test (80 minutes) and an essay question (40 minutes) for which you should write about 600 words. You have to go to a special centre to sit it and it is sat at a computer. No specialist knowledge is required. There is a fee to pay (£40) which will be waived if you cannot afford it. The multiple choice test involves reading a passage and answering some questions about it. Answer all questions, as you are not penalised for wrong answers.

It is very important to familiarise yourself with the test. Go to the LNAT website and practise the questions on www.lnat.ac.uk. The

LNAT can be taken from early September at centres across the country.

You will have to identify main arguments, assumptions in multiple choice questions and the ways in which arguments link together. The essay can be no longer than four A4 typed pages. A good way to practise the essay is to get involved in debating in your school. If your school does not currently have a debating club why not set one up? Your English teacher or Head of Sixth Form may be able to help you. It will enable you to think on your feet. It is very helpful to read the commentary on the sample test on the website and note the hints, tips and insights provided.

Unfortunately, we were unable to obtain an example question for the LNAT, but you can find examples and past papers on its website.

Aptitude test for maths and computer science

For applications to maths; maths with computer science, philosophy or statistics; or computer sciences at Oxford only.

This test will be sat at your school on one day at the end of October or beginning of November. Your school will be sent the papers automatically.

The test lasts two and a half hours. The maths exams are based on C1 and C2 of A level maths and not on further maths at all. It is very important to check you have covered the syllabus. However, you are advised to take as much maths as is offered to you, including STEP or AEA (see below). Go to www.maths.ox.ac.uk/prospective-students/undergraduate/specimen-tests to see the actual syllabus for the exam. Calculators are not permitted.

Physics and maths test for physics

For applications to physics or physics and philosophy at Oxford only.

This is a two-hour test. Calculators are not permitted. You need to revise all the physics and maths that you have learnt at school. Short-listing is largely based on the results of the aptitude tests. It is very important to look at the syllabus: www.physics.ox.ac.uk/admissions/syllabus.htm. The physics course at Oxford is highly mathematical and it is important that you demonstrate strong mathematical ability.

TSA (Thinking Skills Assessment)

For applications to a variety of subjects at both Oxford and Cambridge.

Colleges can use the TSA for any subject. See Tables 4 and 5 above for details. The test is taken at your school and will usually be sat in early November. The test consists of the following sections:

- thinking skills assessment (90 minutes, problem-solving skills)
- writing task (30 minutes, one essay from a choice of three).

The Cambridge Assessment Admissions Test website (www.admissionstests.cambridgeassessment.org.uk) gives useful information about the TSAs at both Oxford and Cambridge. Make sure you look at the specimen tests available.

There are two types of question in the test: critical thinking and problem solving. In the problem-solving category you may have questions that involve sifting through information to identify what is important or questions that want you to find a situation that has a similar structure to another. It is important to have an awareness of the maths you need for the test.

The critical-thinking questions can involve the following:

- summarising the main point
- identifying an assumption
- drawing a conclusion
- considering what weakens an argument
- identifying flaws in an argument
- understanding the structure of an argument
- applying principles.

Each question is worth one mark, but some questions are harder than others. Make sure you move on to the next question if you are stuck.

TSA example questions

Cambridge - Specimen paper section 1 question 3

3 Every year in Britain there are nearly 25,000 car fires, yet it is estimated that only five per cent of motorists travel with a fire extinguisher in their car. If more motorists could be encouraged to carry fire extinguishers then the number of car fires could be considerably reduced.

Which of the following is the best statement of the flaw in the argument above?

A   It ignores the fact that millions of motorists never experience a car fire.
B   It assumes that carrying a fire extinguisher will enable fires to be put out.
C   It implies that the occurrence of car fires is related to the lack of an extinguisher.
D   It overlooks the possibility that fires might not be put out with an extinguisher.
E   It ignores the fact that there are different extinguishers for different kinds of fires.

Oxford - Specimen paper section 2 question 1

1 Privacy is only good because people aren't good. In a perfect world we wouldn't need privacy . . . Is that right?

Source: From the specimen papers available on the Cambridge Assessment website (www.admissionstests.cambridgeassessment.org.uk). Reprinted by permission of the University of Cambridge Local Examinations Syndicate.

STEP (Sixth Term Examination Papers)

For applications to maths at Cambridge.

Cambridge almost always asks for a STEP paper in maths as part of a conditional offer for maths (and maths with physics) and it can also be used as part of a conditional offer for engineering at Churchill and Peterhouse, and for computer science at Magdalene and sometimes natural sciences at Peterhouse. No further mathematical knowledge over and above the core maths A level syllabus is needed for STEP. The exam is taken in June at the same time as your A level. The advantage for Cambridge colleges is that they can read your examination script and therefore assess your strengths (and weaknesses!) in a way that just isn't possible from an A level grade. Cambridge runs a study course to help students from non-selective state schools prepare for the STEP if their school does not offer preparation classes.

STEP example question

STEP 2008 Paper ii Section C: Probability and Statistics.

Question 12.

In the High Court of Farnia, the outcome of each case is determined by three judges: the ass, the beaver and the centaur. Each judge decides its verdict independently. Being simple creatures, they make their decisions entirely at random. Past verdicts show that the ass gives a guilty verdict with probability p, the beaver gives a guilty verdict with probability p/3 and the centaur gives a guilty verdict with probability p2.

Let X be the number of guilty verdicts given by the three judges in a case. Given that E(X) = 4/3, find the value of p.

The probability that a defendant brought to trial is guilty is t. The King pronounces that the defendant is guilty if at least two of the judges give a guilty verdict; otherwise, he pronounces the defendant not guilty. Find the value of t such that the probability that the King pronounces correctly is 1/2.

AEAs (Advanced Extension Awards)

Used only for maths.

Like STEP, AEA requires no additional subject knowledge to your A level syllabus and assesses your ability in critical thinking and logic. It is taken after your A levels. Neither university requires the AEA in Maths as part of their offer, but you are encouraged to take the paper if it is available at your school as they are looked upon favourably as they are known to really stretch you.

Preparation for logic-based tests

To help with preparation for the TSA and LNAT, and the first section of the BMAT, as well as logic problems in the maths exams, it would be wise to look at critical-thinking materials. Look at the past papers and mark schemes for the critical-thinking GCSEs, A levels and AEA that the exam boards AQA and OCR set. Go to:

- www.aqa.org.uk/qual/gce/critical_thinking_new.php
- www.ocr.org.uk/Data/publications/key_documents/AS_A_Level8695.pdf
- www.ocr.org.uk/qualifications/asa_levelgceforfirstteaching2008/critical_thinking/index.html and www.ocr.org.uk/qualifications/aea/critical_thinking/index.html.

Tests for subjects other than the ones covered

If you are applying for any other subjects you will probably have to do an exam directly before your interview. For past papers go to: www.admissions.ox.ac.uk/interviews/tests. However, this list is subject to change, and you must consult the relevant websites regularly to check. If you are in doubt, give the admissions tutor a ring to clarify. Cambridge colleges set their own individual exams. Have a look on the individual colleges' websites for guidance about the exams and/or contact the admissions tutor to ask for sample material. It may be that in addition or as an alternative to an exam, you are given an article to read and discuss in your interview. Be prepared for this and take a highlighter and pen.

Even if you do well in this test (you will probably be told your mark in your interview and your answers may also be discussed) you cannot rest on your laurels. You need to show extra sparkle in the interview as well as having a good mark in the written test. This is the subject of the next chapter.

Checklist

- Find out whether you will have to take a test before your interview and whether you will sit the test in your own school or at an external test centre.
- Prepare for tests by going through past papers.
- Make sure you know the date of your exam.
- Make sure that you are able to read a text, understand it and explain it to someone else, noting the main points of the argument and any assumptions or flaws. You could try reading a newspaper editorial from a good newspaper and explaining it as above to somebody else.

Further reading

- *Critical Thinking and Problem Solving*, Mike Bryon, Kogan Page Ltd, London, 2006 (the ultimate psychometric test book)
- *Critical Thinking: An Introduction*, A. Fisher, Cambridge University Press, Cambridge, 2001
- *Management Level Psychometric and Assessment Tests*, Andrea Shavick, How to Books Ltd, Oxford, 2005
- *Logic*, 2nd revised edition, Willfred Hodges, Penguin Books, London, 2001
- *There are Two Errors in the the Title of This Book*, Robert Martin, Broadview Press, Canada, 1992

- *Practice Tests for Critical Verbal Reasoning: Succeed at Psychometric Testing*, Peter Rhodes, Hodder Arnold, London, 2006
- *Logical Forms*, Mark Sainsbury, Wiley Blackwell, Iowa, 1991
- *Passing the UK Clinical Aptitude Test (UKCAT) and BMAT*, 2nd revised edition, F. Taylor, R. Hutton and G. Hutton, Law Matters Publishing, 2007

Websites

For questions similar to the critical thinking components of BMAT, ELAT, HAT, LNAT, TSA (although these ones are used for graduate recruitment) go to:

- www.shl.com/shl/en-int/candidatehelpline
- www.shldirect.com/example_questions.html.

08

The interview

Many universities do not interview candidates at all. They judge you entirely on your predicted grades, reference and Personal Statement. However, Oxford and Cambridge will never offer you a place without an interview. (Even if you are unfortunate enough to be too ill to attend in person, you will have to do a telephone interview, often interacting with resources on the internet.) Before you begin to panic, it is important, however, to remember that the interview is only *one* part of the application process. Both universities take into account so many other things. It is helpful to remind yourself of what these are:

- A level results
- GCSE results
- reference
- Personal Statement
- written work sent in
- tests sat before interview or at interview.

So don't forget that all of these things are important too. It is theoretically possible to score very highly in all of the aspects in the list above but perform poorly at interview, yet still be offered a place. And this is because, at the risk of repeating myself, it's only part of the process. So now we have got that into perspective hopefully, let's see if we can help you to perform to the best of your abilities.

Why are you being interviewed?

The interviewers are trying to assess your academic potential. They want to know what sort of student you are and what you will be like on their course. The Oxbridge interview is your chance to show that you are more than simply the sum of your qualifications and that you know more than how to revise well and work hard. It allows the interviewers, some of whom will teach you during your three or four years there, to discover your future academic potential. The interviewers are looking to see how much you have absorbed already from your academic work and to see how you use what you know. They are certainly not looking for candidates who already know half the degree course before they have even done their A levels. Rather, they want to know what you can do with what you have already got. You should not therefore be worried about the fact that you know very few technical legal terms or are unsure as to exactly how the latest computer chip works. They are not looking for a walking encyclopaedia. On the other hand, your interest in the subject should mean that you have done some investigation into recent studies or issues in your chosen subject and can discuss them to some extent.

The interview format

The number and format of the interview(s) will vary from college to college so it is not possible to predict this. Be prepared for the following when you arrive.

Reading material

You may be asked to read through something shortly before your interview with a view to discussing it once you are with the interviewers. This could be a poem, a newspaper article, a law report, a graph; the list is endless. Do not worry if it is not something which you have seen or studied before. Try to work out what it is, where it is from, who it is by or what you know that has similarities to it. Then you need to try to think about what sort of questions you may be asked on it.

Further reading material

As above, you may be asked to read through something, but whilst you are in the interview with the interviewers looking at you. This can seem somewhat daunting and you may try to rush through your reading in order to answer their questions. Don't: stay calm and read carefully. Try to recognise something and if you don't, tell them so, but try to tell them if, as mentioned above, there is some similarity with another poem or graph you have studied.

General interview

Not all colleges will give you an admissions interview but if they do, you can expect them to focus on the more general aspects of you and your application, not necessarily your abilities within your chosen subject. They may ask about extra-curricular activities that you are currently doing and may enquire as to what activities you hope to undertake at university. But do be aware that they could ask something broad about your interest in your subject too.

Subject interview

This is the hardest to predict in terms of its format and quantity. You may only have one interview, but you could have up to three. You may have one interviewer in one interview but a panel in another. Where you have more than one interviewer, be aware of your eye contact. When answering a question, look mostly at the person who asked the question, but look from time to time at the others as well. Don't ignore anyone! This will be the interview where your subject understanding will be tested and your potential assessed.

What do they want to see?

The interviewers want to see a clear interest on your part in your chosen degree subject. Let's call it passion if you like. They want to see true enthusiasm and excitement for what you plan to read. If you know in your heart of hearts that you don't have this level of excitement about your subject, I do recommend that you think again about an application to one of these universities, where they are impressed by people who are excited. Spending three years or more in a heady academic environment is no fun when you are not particularly interested in your work. Remember that passionate attachment to a subject can be shown by your own reactions to questions but also in your preparation and reading. To say that you are passionate about the author Gabriel García Márquez, but to have only read three of his novels does not show true passion. It shows someone who won't keep up with the pace of work expected at either university.

They look for people who are able to show analytical ability, clarity of thought and intellectual flexibility. By this latter phrase, I mean that they want to see that you are willing to listen to other arguments and to see the strength in other ideas, as well as having the confidence to say once in a while that you are wrong! They want to see students who are looking to learn and discuss complex ideas and they want people who are excited by exploration. They don't want students who will learn arguments off by heart. Those who succeed are people who show that they have the potential to take their mind down winding intellectual roads which are open to new ideas.

They will be expecting you to have a good understanding of relevant material that you have studied so far at A level. They will be more interested in your grasp of first principles than your memory for facts. They will expect you to have researched at least one or two areas beyond A level, and they will expect you to have done some research on your proposed degree subject and to be able to talk about it analytically and critically. If you can use some technical vocabulary (correctly), you will find that this is a great advantage. They will also be looking for your ability to think on your feet. Finally, they will expect you to be able to remember what you wrote in your written tests and to be able to expand on any written material submitted in advance of the interviews.

How to prepare

All these themes are more or less predictable and you can prepare for them. It is remarkable how far preparation and practice can take you, and even more remarkable how little preparation some of your competitors will have done. Start with the following.

- Ask yourself what aspects of the subject attract you to it.
- Ensure that you are fully up to speed on all the topics you have so far covered in your A levels.
- Make yourself aware of any important recent developments in your chosen subject.
- Think about the reason why your subject is studied.
- Think about your subject's broader application in the real world. How relevant is it to everyday life?
- Go through the prospectus and make sure that you know the course that is on offer. Be prepared to go into some detail as to the aspects of it which have attracted you.
- On the major topics within your subject, look at the common arguments on both sides. Make sure you understand them all and know which one you agree with. Be prepared to justify your choice.

Candidates should be intellectually robust, inquisitive and ambitious.

Admissions Tutor, Cambridge

What can you expect in an interview?

- *Structured but informal discussion.*
- *Challenging and open-ended questions.*
- *Questions on school work outside of your comfort zone.*
- *Problem solving/critical thinking.*

Admissions Tutor, Cambridge

At the interview

Show them what you know . . .

The key here is, when answering their questions, to think aloud as much as possible. If you need a bit more time to think or you did not quite get your head around the question, simply say, 'I'm sorry, would you mind repeating the question?' or 'Am I right in thinking that what you are getting at is . . .?'. Do not be afraid to ask for clarification. It shows a willingness to engage with the question and the quest for clarity is itself a good thing and it demonstrates that you are precise and accurate.

Thinking aloud means going through the thought process out loud. It is a bit like when you are asked to show all your workings in a maths calculation instead of just writing down the answer. The advantage to thinking aloud is that if you go wrong somewhere the interviewer might say 'Are you sure about that?'. If necessary you can always ask for a piece of paper to do a calculation: this is probably very useful in physics for jotting down an equation or biology for drawing a diagram of a cell. Asking for things such as a piece of paper shows confidence in yourself. It shows that you are in control of your ideas and are able to interact with the tutors, regardless of their academic status, which is important, as you will have to interact with them regularly if you get in.

> My last interview was the most challenging of the four interviews
> I had, simply because of the way in which I was interviewed.
> There were two professors, who bombarded me with a series
> of questions in quick succession, constantly interrupting my
> answers to ask why I had said that, where I was getting my
> evidence from and could I give more examples of the point I
> was making.
>
> **Oxford Applicant**

If you are applying for a humanities course, such as PPE, to show you are thinking aloud you could say: 'Well, I would go about this question by breaking the problem down into stages, first I would consider . . .'. As well as showing that you are thinking logically and considering the problem without giving a knee-jerk answer, it also buys you some more time for your brain to tick things over. Don't be afraid to give an answer even if you think it is wrong (of course it is better to give one that is right!). Giving no answer at all shows you are not able to think on your feet or be innovative. Giving an answer, in stages, allows the interviewer to prompt you at the stage where you may be going wrong, giving you the maximum chance of giving an answer in the right ball park. In most subjects, there is no right or wrong answer anyway, and it is the logic you employ that is of interest to the interviewers.

How to answer a difficult question

First of all, stay calm and remember exactly what it is that the interviewers are trying to achieve. They are not primarily trying to find out what facts you know. They are endeavouring to find out if you have an enquiring mind and if you can apply first principles and the facts that you do know to new problems. Let us take a question which has been asked at a past Oxbridge interview and go through a possible sequence which might be used in order to answer it.

Should judges be elected?

This is a question which appears to require a definitive answer. Immediately you should be aware that you will need to look at all sides of the argument, whether you agree with them or not, with the final aim of coming down on a particular side if you can. Are there any words in the question which might need clarification? For example, does the word 'elected' refer to election by the public or by other judges or even by politicians? Start by discussing this. As you speak you are giving yourself both clarification of the issue and more time to think. Identify the main issues which would arise were judges to be elected. Point out the advantages and disadvantages, all the time putting forward an opinion of your own, and if you have none, put forward those which are generally held, if you know them.

It may be impossible for you to come up with an answer you feel happy with. In which case, say so. Explain that you feel the arguments for and against are all persuasive and you do not therefore feel able to fully answer the question. If, however, you do have an opinion as to the 'correct' answer, give it, ensuring that you reiterate the arguments to back up your choice.

The interview is trying to recreate a supervision. If you handle a question badly acknowledge it and move on. What you say is more important than how you say it.

Admissions Tutor, Cambridge

What to do if you can't answer the question

Above all, do not panic!

Start by identifying what it is about the question that has stopped you in your tracks. Is it that you do not understand the question itself? If so, ask for it to be repeated. If you have no knowledge whatsoever of the topic to which the question refers, ascertain whether there is a related topic about which you do feel confident and say to the interviewer: 'I do not know very much about that particular topic but it seems quite similar to . . .', and then go on to discuss that. You can only really do this if there is some relevance in the topic you are trying to lead them to. You can to some extent steer the interview to your advantage and show them where you can shine. Where this is not possible, use the approach described above for a difficult question and this will get you some of the way at least. Whatever you do though, don't pretend that you know what you are talking about when you do not have a clue. Far better to be honest and admit your difficulties than to try to pull the wool over your interviewers' eyes. It will invariably fail, as these people are leading academics in their chosen field. You will often find that when you are struggling you will be prompted and this will be all that you need to get back on track.

Some real interview experiences

The following accounts are of interviews which students have actually attended. They are from current and ex-students at the school at which the author works.

Adam (Economics — Cambridge)

Two weeks before my interview I was sent an interview pack from Cambridge which contained an article that I read in advance of the interview, a few maps of the college and of Cambridge, some information about the interviews and a food voucher for the food hall.

My interview was at midday. I could have stayed over the night before but I live close so I did not. There were no designated student helpers and I got a bit lost in the college (it is very large) so I asked some people for help and directions. I would recommend going to the Porter's Lodge if you get very lost and they will direct you.

My first interview was the specialist interview for Economics. I was interviewed by two fellows, who invited me to sit down on a couch as I entered the room where the interview took place. One interviewer sat directly in front of me and the other sat at a desk looking to the side. The interviewer who sat in front of me was the main interviewer, as the other interviewer hardly ever intervened and just took notes diligently. The interview started with the principal interviewer asking me about what current events in the news had interested me most. I responded by talking about Northern Rock. She asked me why I was interested in what was happening at the time with Northern Rock. I told her that it stemmed from my great interest in Economics and related it to out-of-class reading I had done not only on the subject of Economics but on banking systems. The interview continued in that same tone and style. It was a very sober, tense environment. The interview was very formal and no time was lost on discussions that did not relate to Economics.

I was sent an article a couple of weeks prior to the interview. And I was asked a few questions on it. The answers basically related back to my A level knowledge of the subject. Then I was given a paragraph on Economics and was told to comment on it. The comment could be anything I wanted to say or thought about the paragraph. It had some errors, not grammatical, but rested on dubious theory such as 'if you raise taxes, people will spend more', whereas I have been taught that if you raise taxes people will spend less.

Then they asked me a mathematical problem. They gave me a whiteboard to solve it on. It was a geometric problem. The problem was that there were two pieces of carpet and you had to cover an entire room with those two pieces of carpet. The trick was you could only do one cut. This seemed to me to be impossible. I was told to do what I could and I talked through the logic of finding the solution to that problem. I was stopped after around 30 seconds. After the maths question, the interviewers asked me if I had any questions. I asked them about fiscal policy and we engaged in a small discussion and then the interview came to an end.

My general interview was very relaxed. The admissions tutor asked me very general questions such as 'Why Cambridge?', 'Why this college?'. I was asked questions such as 'Tell me five words your friends would use to describe you'. I was also told to describe an object as if I was on the telephone with the admissions tutor and they could not see the object. After I described the object he asked me why I thought he asked me that. The off-beat, laid-back style characterised the interview. It was a very pleasant experience. The interviewer's questions were either very general and expected or very diverse, unusual and startling.

Comment
Note how the interviewer has tried to find out if Adam could look beyond the question and analyse why it had been asked. Very often the question itself is not as interesting as the reason why it has been asked.

Melissa (Human Sciences — Oxford)

I had two interviews which seemed to me more like discussions than any sort of interrogation, as I had been led to believe they would be by my school. I had undertaken a mock interview in order to prepare and I was pleased that I had because its style had prepared me for the worst! When I arrived, the undergraduates at the college were incredibly helpful, as they were able to give me an insight into what my interviewers were like and they told me what little they could remember of their own interviews too.

The first interview lasted around 30 minutes and took place in an office just big enough for the two of us. The interviewer started by telling me about himself and some recent research he had been doing – I was so shocked by this as I had expected everything to be about me! It was very effective, though, as it calmed me down as it was so like an ordinary conversation. He then proceeded to ask me why I had chosen this subject over others that might have seemed more obvious for someone with my A levels. We then moved on to some technical questions, one of which involved me commenting on a graph portraying the age of death in certain countries. As I had not looked at this beforehand I had to think on my feet. He had looked at the work I had sent in, and asked me to look at how one of the essays related to the subject I was applying for. He let me talk on about this for what seemed like ages and asked me lots about it. He seemed interested but maybe he was just a good actor!

In the second interview, I felt far more challenged but not in a confrontational way. When I was asked a question and gave an answer the interviewer would ask me yet another question on my answer in order to take me deeper into the subject matter. A common question she asked was 'Why?'. It was a very stimulating interview and she seemed genuinely interested in what I had to say. Although I think I tackled much of it well on my own I do think that my better analysis was prompted by her questions and the general discussion.

Both the interviewers were very hospitable and seemed to be keen to find my strengths rather than my weaknesses. On the whole, I suppose I actually enjoyed the experience!

Comment
It is worth noting that had Melissa not prepared thoroughly she would not have been able to talk on her essay or for long! It is imperative that you are completely familiar with any work which is sent in to the admissions tutor. Look at any angles which were not covered in the title and try to foresee questions which could commonly arise from it. Also, don't worry if the interviewer has to keep digging to get the 'correct' answer from you. The idea that your best answers come out when your are challenged by the interviewer goes to the heart of the interview process.

Grace (History – Oxford)

When I arrived at Oxford for the interview I was terribly nervous. I was taken through to a small study where two female professors were sitting. As soon as I walked in, I could sense that the atmosphere was much more relaxed than I had imagined it would be. The initial questions they asked me were drawn from points I had made in my Personal Statement, many of them about the Holy Grail. This immediately made me feel more relaxed, as I was confident about being able to support what I had written in my Personal Statement.

It was clear to me that they were not trying to trick me by asking questions about historical periods I hadn't covered. They were far more interested in the periods I had covered and were trying to engage me in debate by contradicting a number of the arguments I put forward in response to their questions.

After around 20 minutes, the questions became focused on an essay I had submitted prior to the interview. The questions were designed to make me look at alternative arguments to those I had used in my essay, and they made me question whether my arguments were right. However, when one of the interviewers asked me a question that seemed to have numerous correct answers, I realised that they were more interested in my ability to analyse different points of view.

I enjoyed my interview but I was not offered a place.

Comment

When an interview seems to be rather one tracked, it is acceptable for an interviewee to attempt to steer the conversation towards a related but different topic by saying, for example, 'Yes, I have looked into that but I have found that my interest lies more in . . .'.

Are there any differences between the interviews at the two universities? Read the following two interviews, both for languages, and see if you can discern any differences.

Imogen (French and Italian – Oxford)

I was called approximately 10 days before my provisional date, but the letter did nothing except confirm that I had been called. There were no times or details given. Upon arrival at Oxford, the night before the interviews began, I learnt that the next day I had a language test and an Italian interview, and a French interview the following day.

Oxford prefers not to allow candidates to make their own way to interviews, in case they get lost, so each college has a general waiting room and a group of current undergraduate helpers to accompany everyone. On the morning of the test, all the modern linguists gathered in the waiting room, and we were shown to classrooms where we had to take a grammar test in each of the languages we were applying for, except those we were intending to study ab initio (from scratch). I therefore sat tests in French and Italian, lasting an hour in total, and consisting of translation and multiple choice.

My Italian interview took place at Balliol (I applied to St Anne's), because there is no Italian fellow at St Anne's. A student helper took me to Balliol, and I was given an Italian poem to look at. This was discussed in my interview, which was conducted by only one interviewer, and I was then asked to recount my Personal Statement, because he hadn't seen it. We then discussed various books I have read and, surprisingly, did not speak any Italian.

The next morning I had a French interview at St Anne's, which was conducted by three interviewers. Again I was given a passage to read, again in English, which was discussed with one of the interviewers. There was a conversation in French with a second interviewer, which covered some literature and my reasons for studying French. Last, the third interviewer asked some slightly more in-depth questions about the importance of literature, and the relationship between literature and philosophy (I had made some references to philosophy in my Personal Statement).

I had been told that I would be allowed to leave Oxford at 10 a.m. the following morning, but that some candidates would be required to stay until later the next day to attend interviews at other colleges, to which they had been pooled. This is because the Oxford pooling system is different to that of Cambridge, in that it takes place before any firm offers or rejections are made. It is also possible to have an interview at a college to which you have been pooled, and then still be made an offer by the original college to which you applied. I was not one of these 'pooled' candidates. Indeed, none of the candidates at my particular college was pooled, and we were all allowed to go home.

Inside the actual interview — Italian 1 (one interviewer)
This was a very strange interview. I was given an Italian poem ('Canzonetta sulle sirene catodiche' by Magrelli) to read and make notes on before I was called in.

- I had to describe aspects of the poem which I found interesting.
- I was then asked to summarise my Personal Statement as he hadn't seen it before.
- Then he asked me why I thought that Primo Levi was a good writer, told me that his book was originally rejected by Natalia Ginzburg and asked what I felt about that.
- The conversation then moved on to Dante, and he wanted to know how I had approached my study of *L'Inferno*, and which of the *canti* I had enjoyed.
- I was then given the opportunity to ask him a question.

There was no Italian conversation.

Inside the actual interview – Italian 2 (two interviewers)
I was given a poem in English.

- Again, the poem was discussed in depth, but this time I was pushed to interpret bits which were harder to understand, rather than just comment on bits I liked.
- The interviewer then picked up on the Primo Levi in my Personal Statement, and asked me what I thought of the quote 'After Auschwitz, no more poetry', with reference to the philosophy I studied at school.
- There was a brief conversation in Italian, focusing on current affairs and places I had visited in Italy.
- Again I was allowed to ask a question.

Inside the actual interview – French 1 (three interviewers)
The passage was in English, it was an extract from the works of Edgar Allen Poe.

- I was asked questions about the tone of the passage, what situation I thought the extract was taken from and how I felt the episode would conclude.
- French conversation – why I wanted to study French as opposed to any other language, what I felt the themes were in the film *Jules et Jim* by Francois Truffaut (the essay I sent up was based on this film) and what I felt the film said about the difference between the French and the Germans during the war.
- I was asked a series of questions, including: Why is it important to study literature? What is the difference between literature and philosophy? What French book had I recently read that I enjoyed? I talked about *La Princesse de Cleves*.

Inside the actual interview – French 2 (two interviewers)
The poem was in French. There was a note at the top saying that I should try to understand the poem, but not worry if I didn't know all the vocabulary, because I would be asked which bits of the poem I found most interesting and was not expected to understand it all.

- However, I was then fired a series of questions on every verse of the poem, and interrupted during every answer to be further questioned on why I thought that, where I was getting my information from, and could I give more examples to back up my point. Luckily, I had been placed in a library to read through the passage, and so had looked up all the unfamiliar vocabulary. Moral of the story – don't believe the kindly worded instructions!

- One of the interviewers then said he was intrigued as to my interest in Ronsard, and we discussed where the major Petrarchian influences were in the poetry.
- Then followed French conversation where I had to talk about my work placement in Le Touquet, and what I thought the differences were between French and British holidaymakers.

Madeleine (Modern and Medieval Languages — Cambridge)

Shortly after I had sent off my UCAS form, Cambridge contacted me by letter to give me details of the written work they required, which in my case was two essays; one for Latin and one for Italian. I therefore wrote a discursive essay in English for the Latin requirement, and a short essay based on an A level topic in Italian. These essays were due early in November.

I was then called to interview, again by letter, which arrived roughly halfway through November, and was told all the details and times of the tests and interviews I would be expected to sit, which all took place on one day in the first half of December.

I stayed in college the night before my interviews, due to an early start the next day, which I would highly recommend as it gives one the opportunity to get used to the surroundings, talk to current students and it means that it isn't a great rush in the morning before interview. I had to sit a test first, and as a language applicant I had to choose one of my languages in which to answer. In my case, it had to be Italian, but as it turned out, very little of the test was actually in the foreign language. There was a passage to be read, in English, which I had to summarise in a foreign language (Italian), and then I had to answer a very broad essay question in English. The test lasted an hour.

My first interview was a couple of hours later, so I took the opportunity to have lunch with some friends who were also applying to other colleges, whilst making sure I left myself plenty of time to get to the interview, which was for the Latin side of my application. I was given some Latin poetry to read, try to understand and analyse, and this was then discussed in the interview. I was also questioned about the essay I had sent up, and was given some general questions about why I had applied for the course and what my gap year plans were. In this particular interview, there were two interviewers.

Following this was my Italian interview, which was conducted by one person only. Again, I was given a passage to try to understand and talk about, and then we discussed the literature that I was studying for my A2. Finally, she asked me a couple of questions in Italian to test my standard of speaking, focusing on where I had visited in Italy.

After this, I was free to leave, with nothing else to do but wait for the result. At Cambridge the results are all given out on one day, shortly after Christmas, and this date is stated in advance. There will be one of three possible results given on this day, either an acceptance, a rejection or the news that you have been placed in the 'winter pool', which means that there is a possibility that another college will accept you, based on the strength of your UCAS form. Acceptance or rejection from this pool can be held until as late as the end of January, during which time there is the possibility of being called for further interviewing.

Inside the actual interview — Latin (two interviewers)

I was given a 20-line passage of Ovid's *Metamorphoses*, about half an hour before the start of the interview, and left in the library to look at it. I was then escorted up to the interview room. I was addressed first by the general admissions tutor for Modern and Medieval Languages, who asked me what had brought me to my choice of languages (Latin and Italian), and which aspects of the course at Cambridge appealed. She then asked me lots of questions about the gap year I intended to take, how I thought it would be beneficial to me and how I planned to keep my study skills alive whilst I was away.

The rest of the interview was conducted by the Latin lecturer, who started by asking me some grammatical questions about the passage I had looked at. I had to translate bits of it, and then identify some literary techniques used to enhance the meaning. We then talked about the passage in general, focusing more on the themes and general storyline. He then mentioned the essay I had sent up, which was an analysis of Book I of Virgil's *Aeneid*. He questioned me quite closely on one comment I had made, so closely that the point came where I could no longer defend myself!

We discussed my Personal Statement, in particular the references I had made to Linear B, an ancient Mycenaean language, and I was asked what reading I had done to develop this unusual interest. Last, he asked me to imagine that I was talking to someone who had never studied Classics before, and to recommend them one book to read and explain my choice.

Inside the actual interview — Italian (one interviewer)

There was no pre-reading for this interview, I went straight in. The interview began with some questions on my background in Italian. We then moved swiftly on to literature, in particular Pirandello's *Sei Personaggi in Cerca d'Autore*, which I had just begun at school. She asked me what I thought of it so far, and how I thought it might develop. She then produced a short text for me to look at. I read it aloud so that she could hear my accent, and she asked me to translate what I could of it. It was a very abstract opening to a novel (*Se Una Notte D'Inverno Un Viaggiatore* by Italo Calvino), and as the Pirandello play mentioned above is also quite abstract, we compared the two.

Afterwards, we talked in Italian for a bit, focusing on places I had been in Italy and current affairs (including some basics such as who the Prime Minister of Italy is etc.) This interview struck me as being very informal, that is, we did not sit across from each other, but at a small table, and she did not take any notes.

Differences between Oxford and Cambridge interview processes

Although there are some logistical differences between Oxford and Cambridge interviews, the style of the actual interviews is very similar. However, within the universities, different colleges have different interview practices and you should look at the individual college websites for further information.

Here is a summary of the main differences between the two universities.

- Cambridge interviews span one day only, Oxford between two and five.
- At Oxford it is possible to have interviews at other colleges through the pooling system (so bring an umbrella!), but at Cambridge if your first choice college pools you for another college to consider, any further interview would take place in January. See page 107 for an explanation of the pooling system.
- Cambridge will tell you your interview date well in advance, Oxford will give you short notice, and expect you to know when to arrive by the 'provisional date' section in the prospectus. Oxford reserves the right to call a candidate to interview any time up until a week before the provisional date given.
- Cambridge makes known individual interview start times and locations in advance, Oxford does not.
- The Oxford pooling is done 'pre-offer', Cambridge conducts pooling afterwards.
- Oxford will inform you of its decision before Christmas, Cambridge after.

Interview tips

- Try to smile and look alert but relaxed.
- Remember: turn off your mobile phone – even though it can happen to the best of us, it always seems rude when a mobile phone rings.

103

- You may be given a text to consider directly before your interview. Make sure you have a pen and highlighter with you and actively read the text by underlining relevant phrases or words and writing notes and question marks in the margins.
- Smile and walk with purpose into the interview room.
- Have a firm handshake.
- Prepare questions you want to ask.
- Be punctual and allow plenty of time for the journey. It is useful to have a contact number in the event that you may be delayed.

What shall I wear?

The interviews take place in December, and both Oxford and Cambridge can be very cold, so make sure you wear layers – take an extra jumper or cardigan.

For boys it's probably unnecessary to wear a suit, and if you're not used to wearing one, it may feel so uncomfortable as to be a distraction. Decent trousers and a shirt will suffice, but a tie is not needed. Academics are not known to be the most smartly dressed people but you need to look presentable; this means you need to be clean (no mud under your fingernails), shaven, make sure you hair is reasonably kempt (even if the latest style is 'bedhead'). No jewellery unless you are extremely attached to it, although a watch is a good idea. Clean shoes. You want to be bright eyed, so go to bed early for the whole week before your interview. Girls – this is probably not the time to turn up in jeans and your boyfriend's jumper. Similarly it is unnecessarily formal to wear a suit. A smart skirt or trousers with a modest top will do. This is not the time to wear your sexiest knee-high boots or your lowest neckline. It is sad that women are judged on what they wear and although there is no reason why an intelligent girl should not be sexy, don't prove the point at the interview. You are dressing up as a very clever, very articulate young woman. If you want to wear a skirt, make sure it is at least knee length. The point is, your clothes should not speak louder than you. Your clothes should complement you.

Body language

Although it is natural in an interview situation, try not to sit there with your arms crossed. It is a very defensive position and screams out 'no confidence'. Make an effort to sit with your arms open, resting on the arms of the chair or on your lap. When you speak it is a good idea to gesticulate with your arms as it adds expression. However, don't overdo it. Don't bite your nails or fiddle with your hair. Often we exhibit certain mannerisms when we are thinking. It may be worth getting someone to video you when you talk to see if you have some unconscious mannerisms that are unflattering. Your school may offer this as part of a mock interview programme, but if they don't, ask them if they will. Lean forwards, not back, and sit up straight – to show interest. Speak slowly. We speak much more quickly than we realise – so slow down! Do not speak in a monotone – moderate your voice by using highs and lows. Do not fold your arms or cross your legs – these are defensive gestures that suggest you are scared to open up.

Preparation

Revise all your A level subjects, particularly the one which you are planning to study at university – if this is applicable. However, it is important to know all your A level subjects in depth as you will look pretty silly if they ask you a bog-standard A level question and you don't know the answer. In any case, you need to revise for your A levels so there is no loss in doing some revision beforehand. Remember that you may be asked about the content of your Personal Statement, so take a copy with you to review the night before your interview.

Your school can probably arrange for you to have a mock interview with someone whom you do not know. The interviewer should have a copy of your Personal Statement and reference. It is a good idea to have a mock interview as it allows you to gauge how much time to spend answering questions, lets you consider if you are speaking too quickly and in general it gives you a dry run, as for many of you, your Oxbridge interview will be your first real interview. However, it is important not to be over-prepared, as you will sound 'stale' in your interview.

> *We keep an eye out for candidates who are determined to make their prepared point. Students should not be overly or inadequately prepared for interview.*
> **Admissions Tutor, Cambridge**

Typical problems at interview:

Applicants are:

- *too eager to agree/not keen to discuss/debate*
- *well informed but cautious or uncritical in thinking*
- *had difficulty when challenged to think for self*
- *reluctant to engage with the unfamiliar*
- *jump into answers without listening.*
> **Admissions Tutor, Cambridge**

So what are the actual arrangements?

The college will give you an itinerary either when you arrive or in advance. It will detail everything. There will be a certain amount of waiting around and it is advisable to bring a book (that extra book you never got round to reading about your subject that you wrote about in your Personal Statement).

> I had a short waiting time in the JCR before my first interview at 10 a.m. I then had a break of about two hours before my next interview. I spent that in the JCR reading newspapers.
>
> **Cambridge Applicant**

Where do we eat?

Meals (breakfast, lunch and dinner) in college tend be served in large 'halls', meaning dining halls. At the older colleges, these are steeped in tradition – they may be lined in oak panelling and have portraits of famous alumni hung on the wall. The dining hall in *Harry Potter* was filmed in the hall of Christ Church, Oxford so watch it to get an idea. But all colleges are different and you will find halls quite different at the newer colleges. The tables are probably long tables and at some colleges you will be served your entire meal and at others it will be self-service. You will be sitting with other (nervous) candidates, but relax and try to enjoy the company of your peers. It is easy to be intimidated by these halls but remember, Oxford and Cambridge are very old institutions, and it should not be surprising that their halls are so grand. It is all part of the experience.

Meals are served at set times in colleges. It may be that when you arrive you have already missed lunch or dinner. There are two options at this point. Either ask one of the student helpers where the JCR is where you may be able to buy a sandwich, or go outside into town. It's easy to forget that Oxford and Cambridge are towns in their own right – they have all the high street shops that you are used to!

No one will tell you when to go to bed and no doubt the student helpers will show you where the college bar is after dinner. It might be nice to have a look, but I would refrain from drinking. Don't worry about looking like a nerd, just say 'I am a bit nervous and think I should have an early night'. Remember, you are going for the fresh-eyed look. Furthermore, it would create a very bad impression to smell of alcohol the next day.

Accommodation

Very often, for Oxford interviews (but not for Cambridge interviews) you will have to stay over in the college for a number of nights. Everything Is paid for: all meals and accommodation. You simply need to take an overnight bag and your interview clothes. You may need to take a few shirts or tops, as it may be that you have several interviews on different days. Many of the rooms will have en suite facilities (a shower or toilet in your room). Bring a towel. It may be that you are housed in an old-fashioned block, in which case the showers are in cubicles in a general shower room. People who have been to boarding school are used to these living arrangements but for people who have not lived away from home it may be a new experience – nothing to worry about though.

Checklist of things to bring

- Photocopies of your Personal Statement and essays
- Overnight toiletries and towel
- Interview clothes
- Hairdryer
- Umbrella
- Money for emergencies
- Pens and a highlighter
- Phone number of tutor or college
- Note book.

Why can't Oxford tell me exactly how long I will be staying?

Your interview letter may say that you may have to stay for up to four days. The reason is that one of your interviews may be on day one and one may be on day two. Also you may have an exam to do on one day and an interview on another. At this point, we need to discuss the pooling system and this is one of the main differences between the Oxford and Cambridge entrance systems.

The pool

Each college can only accept a certain number of candidates. If the college has already found the students it wants to fill its places but thinks that you are an excellent candidate, it puts you into the 'pool' so that other colleges can pick you to interview if they have not filled their quota of places. You have a very good chance of getting in if you have been pooled, so you don't need to be disappointed if this happens to you. You also may still get in to your first choice of college.

3000 offers are made by preference colleges, 600–700 offers are made through the pool.

Admissions Tutor, Cambridge

In your college in Oxford, a list will go up on the notice board detailing who has been pooled and where you should go and what time (see map of Oxford and Cambridge at back). If your name is on this list you will have to take yourself to the appropriate college. Get one of the student helpers to tell you where it is. The pool at Cambridge is done after interviews, so you will be told by letter if you have been pooled to another college. You may be asked to attend another interview at the college to which you have been pooled, but it may be that you are offered a place without a further interview. If you do have to attend another interview, it will take place in early January (see Figure 1).

Relieved that my interviews were over for that day, I walked slowly back to St Anne's, but upon arrival I learnt that it is very important to check the notice board in the waiting room frequently, because there was a notice up saying that I had been asked to go for an interview at Hertford College.

Oxford Applicant

Around one in five applicants are pooled and of these around one in four receives an offer.

Cambridge Admissions webpages

How to get there

Travel information is available on the websites for Oxford and Cambridge. Also check out www.nationalexpress.com and www.nationalrail.co.uk.

I advise not to drive yourself as there is nowhere to park inside the city centres (unless you park in the Park and Ride car parks, which are several miles outside the centre, requiring a bus ride to the centre). If someone is giving you a lift, you will have to say goodbye in the car as there is no parking.

Do leave plenty of time to get there. If you are really early you can wander round the shops or have a look at some of the other colleges – there is lots to do and see in Oxford and Cambridge.

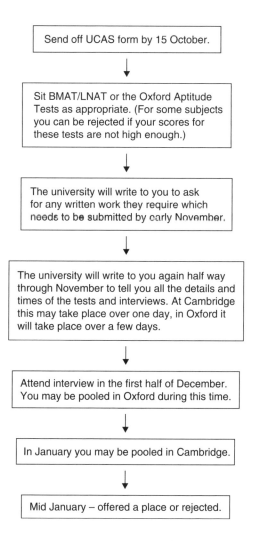

Send off UCAS form by 15 October.

Sit BMAT/LNAT or the Oxford Aptitude Tests as appropriate. (For some subjects you can be rejected if your scores for these tests are not high enough.)

The university will write to you to ask for any written work they require which needs to be submitted by early November.

The university will write to you again half way through November to tell you all the details and times of the tests and interviews. At Cambridge this may take place over one day, in Oxford it will take place over a few days.

Attend interview in the first half of December. You may be pooled in Oxford during this time.

In January you may be pooled in Cambridge.

Mid January – offered a place or rejected.

Interview questions

The following are questions which have been asked at Oxford and Cambridge interviews in the last few years. The specialist interview questions have been divided by subject, and for brevity, the topic is sometimes given rather than the whole series of questions which were asked. Several of the questions were linked to material on the written tests. Remember that it is pointless to try to mug up responses to all of these questions. They are here to give you a general flavour of the types of questions which might be asked and to enable you to plan the best method of practising for the task which lies ahead of you.

General interview questions

- Why this college?
- What are you intending to do in your gap year?
- Summarise your Personal Statement.
- Excluding your A level reading, what were the last three books you read?
- I notice that you have a grade B in Biology GCSE. Should we be worried about that?
- Give a critical appraisal of the main broadsheet newspaper that you read.
- What do you regard as your strengths and weaknesses?
- What extra-curricular activities would you pursue at this college?
- Do you realise that you have applied for the most popular college at this university?
- Why did you make an 'open application'?
- Give us three reasons why we should offer you a place.
- What will you do if we don't?
- What are the synergies, if any, between your three A level subjects/why did you choose your A level subjects?
- So, is it the case that you only want to come to this university but don't care what you do?
- Why did you choose your A level subjects?
- Name one weakness you have and explain how you would rectify it.
- How will this degree help in your chosen career?
- Do you believe that you have an adventurous side?
- Do you find it daunting not knowing what you will be doing in four or five years' time?
- How would your friends describe you?
- Why are you having to retake your A level(s)? What happened last year?

Specialist interview questions

Anthropology/archaeology

- How do you feel about having to study both anthropology and archaeology during your first year before choosing one?
- Name the six major world religions.
- Does Stonehenge mean anything to you?
- What are the problems regarding objectivity in anthropological studies?
- Why do civilisations erect monuments?
- Why should we approach all subjects from a holistic, anthropological perspective?

Art history

- What do we look for when we study art? What are we trying to reveal?
- Comment on this painting on the wall.
- Compare and contrast these three images.
- What exhibitions have you been to recently?
- How can you classify whether a piece of art is successful or not?
- Do we theorise too much about art?
- Why history of art?
- How does history of art help you to break down barriers and communicate with people?
- Does knowing languages help you communicate with the inhabitants of the country?
- Can you compare the study of the Renaissance with that of the French Revolution?
- Apart from your studies, how else might you pursue your interest in art history while at the university?

Biochemistry

- Questions on catalysts, enzymes and the chemistry of the formation of proteins.
- Questions on oxidation, equilibria and interatomic forces.
- Questions on X-ray crystallography.
- Why do you wish to read biochemistry rather than chemistry?
- Current issues in biochemistry.

Biological sciences

- How does the immune system recognise invading pathogens as foreign cells?
- How does a cell stop itself from exploding due to osmosis?
- Why is carbon of such importance in living systems?
- How would you transfer a gene to a plant?
- Explain the mechanism of capillary action.
- What are the advantages of the human genome project?
- How would you locate a gene in a nucleus of a cell for a given characteristic?
- What is the major problem with heart transplants in the receiver?
- How does the transplant receiver respond to foreign heart cells?
- How does the body recognise and distinguish its own cells from the foreign cells after a transplant?

Chemistry

- Questions on organic mechanisms.
- Questions on structure, bonding and energetics.
- Questions on acids and bases.

- Questions on isomerisation.
- Questions on practical chemical analysis.
- See also biochemistry questions.

Classics
- Questions on classical civilisations and literature.
- Why do you think ancient history is important?
- How civilised was the Roman world?
- Apart from your A level texts, what have you read in the original or in translation?

Earth sciences and geology
- Where would you place this rock sample in geological time?
- How would you determine a rock's age?
- Can you integrate this decay curve, and why would the result be useful?
- Questions on chemistry.
- When do you think oil will run out?

Economics
- Explain how the Phillips curve arises.
- Would it be feasible to have an economy which was entirely based on the service sector?
- A man pays for his holiday at a hotel on a tropical island by cheque. He has a top credit rating and rather than cashing it, the hotelier pays a supplier using the same cheque. That supplier does the same thing with one of his suppliers and so on ad infinitum. Who pays for the man's holiday?
- What do you know about the interaction between fiscal and monetary policy?
- I notice that you study mathematics. Can you see how you might derive the profit maximisation formula from first principles?
- Tell me about competition in the television industry.
- How effective is current monetary policy?
- What are your particular interests as regards economics?
- Do you think we should worry about a balance of payments deficit?
- If you were the Chancellor of the Exchequer, how would you maximise tax revenue?
- If you had a fairy godmother who gave you unlimited sums of money, what sort of company would you start and what types of employee would you hire?
- What are the advantages and disadvantages of joining the euro?
- What are the qualities of a good economist?
- Why are you studying Economics A level?

- What would happen to employment and wage rates if the pound depreciated?
- Do you the think the Chinese exchange rate will increase?
- How does the housing market affect inflation?
- How has social mobility changed in recent times?

Engineering

- Questions on mathematics and physics, particularly calculus and mechanics.
- Questions on mathematical derivations, for example, of laws of motion.
- This mechanical system sitting on my desk – how does it work?
- How do aeroplanes fly?
- What is impedance matching and how can it be achieved?
- How do bicycle spokes work?
- How would you divide a tetrahedron into two identical parts?
- What is the total resistance of the tetrahedron if there are resistors of one ohm on each edge?
- Questions on Hooke's law.

English

- What defines a novel as Gothic?
- What is the most important work of literature of the twentieth century?
- Who is your favourite author?
- Do you do any creative writing? Do you keep a diary? Do you write letters?
- Discussion of reading beyond your A level texts.
- Give a review of the last Shakespeare play you saw at the theatre.
- What do you think about the hypothesis that Shakespeare was unusually atheistic for his time?
- Questions on deconstruction of a poem.
- Questions on the use of language.
- Are Iago and Othello good listeners?
- Tell me about the last novel you read.

Geography

- Is geography just a combination of other disciplines?
- Why should it be studied in its own right?
- Would anything remain of geography if we took the notion of place off the syllabus?
- How important is the history of towns when studying settlement patterns?
- Why is climate so unpredictable?
- What is the importance of space in global warming?

- Why do you think people care about human geography more than physical geography?
- What is more important, mapping or computer models?
- If you went to an isolated island to do research on the beach how would you use the local community?
- Analyse a graph about a river. Why are there peaks and troughs?
- Look at a world map showing quality of life indicators. Explain the pattern in terms of two of the indicators.
- See also questions on land economy.

History

- Questions on historical themes and movements.
- How can one define revolution?
- Why did imperialism happen?
- What were the differences between German and Italian unification?
- Who was the greater democrat – Gladstone or Disraeli?
- Was the fall of the Weimar Republic inevitable?
- 'History is the study of the present with the benefit of hindsight.' Do you agree?
- Would history be worth studying if it didn't repeat itself?
- What is the difference between modern history and modern politics?
- What is the position of the individual in history?
- Would you abolish the monarchy for ideological or practical reasons?
- Should we abolish the House of Lords?
- Should we elect the second chamber?
- Why do historians differ in their views on Hitler?
- What skills should a historian have?
- In what periods has the Holy Grail been popular, with whom and why?
- Why do you think the Holy Grail gains more attention during certain periods?
- Why is it important to visit historical sites relevant to the period you are studying?

Human sciences

- Talk about bovine spongiform encephalopathy and its implications, and the role of prions in Creutzfeldt–Jakob disease.
- What causes altitude sickness and how do humans adapt physiologically to high altitudes?
- Tell me about the exploitation of indigenous populations by Westerners.

- Why is statistics a useful subject for human scientists?
- Why are humans so difficult to experiment with?
- How would you design an experiment to determine whether genetics or upbringing is more important?
- What are the scientific implications of globalisation on the world?

Land economy
- Will the UK lose its sovereignty if it joins EMU?
- Will EMU encourage regionalism?
- Will the information technology revolution gradually result in the death of inner cities?
- What has been the effect of the Channel tunnel on surrounding land use?

Law
- Questions on written cases, judgments and arguments.
- Questions on the points of law arising from scenarios – often relating to criminal law or duty of care.
- A cyclist rides the wrong way down a one-way street and a chimney falls on him. What legal proceedings should he take? What if he is riding down a private drive signed 'no trespassing'?
- X intends to poison his wife but accidentally gives the lethal draught to her identical twin. Would you consider this a murder?
- Questions on legal issues, particularly current ones.
- Should stalking be a criminal offence?
- Should judges have a legislative role?
- Do you think that anyone should be able to serve on a jury?
- Should judges be elected?
- Do judges have political bias?
- To what extent do you think the press should be able to release information concerning allegations against someone?
- Is there anything you want to discuss or that you're really interested in?
- Who do you think has the right to decide about euthanasia?
- How does the definition of intent distinguish murder from manslaughter?
- Can you give a definition of murder and manslaughter?
- Should foresight of consequences be considered as intending such consequences?

Material sciences
- Questions on physics, particularly solid materials.
- Questions on mathematics, particularly forces.
- Investigations of sample materials, particularly structure and fractures.

Maths and computation

- Questions (which may become progressively harder) on almost any area of the A level syllabus.

Maths and further maths

- Pure maths questions on integration.
- Applied maths questions on forces.
- Statistics questions on probability.
- Computation questions on iterations, series and computer arithmetic.

Medicine

- What did your work experience teach you about life as a doctor?
- What did you learn about asthma in your work experience on asthma research?
- How have doctors' lives changed in the past 30 years?
- Explain the logic behind the most recent NHS reforms.
- What are the mechanisms underlying diabetes?
- Why is it that cancer cells are more susceptible to destruction by radiation than normal cells?
- How would you determine whether leukaemia patients have contracted the disease because of a nearby nuclear power station?
- What does isometric exercise mean in the context of muscle function?
- What can you tell me about the mechanisms underlying sensory adaptation?
- What is an ECG?
- Why might a general practitioner not prescribe antibiotics to a toddler?
- Why are people anxious before surgery? Is it justifiable?
- How do you deal with stress?
- Questions on gene therapy.
- Questions on the ethics of fetal transplantation.
- Questions on biochemistry and human biology.

Modern languages

- Tests and questions on comprehension and translation.
- Reading tests.
- Questions which focus on the use of language in original texts.
- Describe aspects of a poem [that was given to the candidate before the interview] which you find interesting.
- Interpret a poem, commenting about tone and the context of the poem.
- Why do you want to study your language and not another?

- Why is it important to study literature?
- What is the difference between literature and philosophy?
- What French book have you recently read that you enjoyed?
- French conversation – talking about a work placement.
- Questions on cultural and historical context and genre in European literature.
- How important is analysis of narrative in the study of literature?
- How important is biography in the study of literature?

Natural sciences

- What is an elastic collision?
- What happens when two particles collide – one moving and one stationary?
- What is friction?
- Questions on carboxylic acids.

Oriental studies

- What do you know about the Chinese language and its structure?
- What are the differences between English and any Oriental language with which you are familiar?
- Compare and contrast any ambiguities in the following sentences.
  - ☐ Only suitable magazines are sold here.
  - ☐ Many species inhabit a small space.
  - ☐ He is looking for the man who crashed his car.
- Comment on the following sentences.
  - ☐ He did wrong.
  - ☐ He was wrong.
  - ☐ He was about to do wrong.

Philosophy

- What is philosophy?
- Give examples of philosophical questions.
- Would you agree that if p is true and s believes p, then s knows p?
- Was the question you have just answered about knowing or about the meaning of the word know?
- Comment on this statement(s)/question(s):
  - ☐ I could be dreaming that I am in this interview./I do not know whether I am dreaming or not./Therefore I do not know whether I am in this interview or not.
  - ☐ A machine has a free will.
  - ☐ When I see red, could I be seeing what you see when you see green.

117

- Is it a matter of fact or logic that time travels in one direction only?
- Is our faith in scientific method itself based on scientific method? If so, does it matter?
- I can change my hairstyle and still be me. I can change my political opinions and still be me. I can have a sex change and still be me. What is it then that makes me be me?
- Can it ever be morally excusable to kill someone?

Physics
- Questions on applied mathematics.
- Questions on any aspect of the physics syllabus.
- Questions on mathematical derivations.
- How does glass transmit light?
- How does depressing a piano key make a sound?
- How does the voltage on a capacitor vary if the dielectric gas is ionised?

Politics
- Can you define 'government'. Why do we need governments?
- Can you differentiate between power and authority?
- How can you distinguish between a society, a state and an economy?
- Will Old Labour ever be revived? If so, under what circumstances?
- Why do you think that Communism was unsuccessful in the Russian countryside?
- What would you say to someone who claims that women already have equal opportunities?
- What would you do tomorrow if you were the president of the former Soviet Union?
- How does a democracy work?
- What constitute the ideologies of the extreme right?
- Does the extreme right pose a threat to other less extreme parties?
- What do you think of Labour's discrimination in favour of female parliamentarians?
- How would you improve the comprehensive system of education?

Politics, philosophy and economics
- Define power, authority and influence.
- How important is national identity? What is the Scottish national identity?
- Should medics pay more for their degrees?
- Can you point out the difference in the mentality of Americans in 1760 and 1770?

Psychology

- Questions on neurophysiology.
- Questions on statistics.
- Questions on the experimental elucidation of the mechanisms underlying behaviour.
- Give some examples of why an understanding of chemistry might be important in psychology.
- A new treatment is tested on a group of depressives, who are markedly better in six weeks. Does this show that the treatment was effective?
- There are records of violent crimes that exactly mimic scenes of violence on television. Does this indicate that television causes real violence?
- How would you establish the quietest sound that you can hear as opposed to the quietest sound that you think you can hear?
- Why might one be able to remember items at the beginning and end of an aurally presented list better than items in the middle?
- Could a computer ever feel emotion?
- Is it ethically justifiable to kill animals for the purpose of research?
- What is emotional intelligence?

Social and political sciences

- What is the value of the study of social anthropology?
- Do people need tabloids?
- How would you define terrorism?
- Do you believe in selective education? Are we participating in selective education here?
- Is it possible to pose a sociological problem without sociological bias?
- Does prison work?
- Are MPs only in it for the power?
- What aspects of the subject are you particularly looking forward to studying?

See also questions on politics.

Theology

- Does moral rectitude reside in the agent, the act or its consequences?
- What, if anything, is wrong with voluntary euthanasia?
- What is the best reason that you can think of for believing in the existence of God?
- Do you think that this course could conceivably be persuasive on the issue?
- What relevance does theology have for art history?
- What relevance does archaeology have for theology?

■ Can you comment on the portrayal of Jesus in John versus the other gospels?

Veterinary medicine

■ Should the veterinary profession show positive discrimination in favour of men?

■ Has your work experience influenced your future career aspirations?

■ Can you discuss any aspect of animal physiology which has struck you as contrasting with what you know of human physiology.

■ Would our knowledge of BSE have been of value in controlling foot and mouth disease?

■ Tell me about the biochemistry of DNA.

■ What animal did this skull belong to?

See also questions on biological sciences and chemistry.

Any questions?

You may be asked at the end of your interview if there any questions that you would like to ask the interviewers. 'No thank you' is a perfectly acceptable, no-risk reply. Alternatively, if you wish to ask specific questions about your course or college, which you haven't found answers to despite undertaking all the research suggested, the chances are that the question is worth asking. Don't ask it, though, if you aren't really interested in the answer and couldn't develop the conversation further. One of the braver things that you can do is to ask a question arising from an earlier part of the technical discussion. That can be a good strategy if you felt that you underperformed on a technical question and could have done better. But it can be a risky strategy if the interviewer thinks that you're forcing yourself.

▓ Checklist

■ Go through the practice questions for your subject.

■ Work out your travel arrangements well in advance of your interview.

■ Arrange to have a mock interview at your school.

■ Check out the Oxford podcasts at www.admissions.ox.ac.uk/podcasts/ and in general about interviews at www.admissions.ox.ac.uk/interviews, which will give you more information about Oxford interviews.

■ Check out the film produced by Cambridge at www.cam.uk/interviews.

Getting a conditional offer

Once you have had your interview, you are in the agonising position of having to wait for the result. If you applied to Oxford you will probably know before Christmas and if you applied to Cambridge then you will know in early January. Your offer will be conditional if you have yet to complete your A levels. A conditional offer means that provided you obtain the grades that the college has stipulated, you will be given a place. This can only be confirmed on results day in August. The offer may be a general offer, for example, AAB, or specific, for example, A in chemistry and A and B in two others. A firm or unconditional offer will be made if you already have your A level grades, for example, if you have taken a gap year. This means you have definitely got a place.

Offers vary between colleges. Most colleges make a standard offer of AAA and a few may make an offer of AAB. Some will stipulate that you need to get 90% in certain A level modules. If you are made an offer which only requires you to do three A levels and you are studying for four, you may ask the admissions tutor if you can drop the fourth A level. In some cases, they may agree.

If you did not get an offer of a place then do not despair. Focus on your other universities as you may still be interviewed and you can draw on your experiences to help you. It is fairly natural when you do not get an offer to believe it is because of one of the following reasons:

- I am not intelligent enough
- I answered a question poorly at interview
- my application was not good enough.

To be honest, it is unlikely to be any of the above, although, of course, the second one is a possibility. You may well be aware of this in any case, but one 'wrong' answer at interview is not likely to get you a rejection. Remember that the interview is about looking for your potential, rather than what you already know. As regards your application not being good enough, you may believe that your Personal Statement was not as good as it could have been, or that your teacher's reference was not strong. Don't forget though, that you were offered an interview on the strength of your application among other things, so it is not likely that your application was poor.

It is absolutely vital that you remember that more students apply to Oxford and Cambridge than there are places to be offered. There simply are not enough offers to go round. Simple maths will tell you therefore that somebody has to be rejected. It is a bit like the lottery in that not everybody can win, even though they have put in the same amount of effort as the winner! It is important that you don't make any assumptions about your rejection. If you are keen to know the reasons for your rejection, your school can contact the admissions officer of the college to which you applied and can ask for some feedback. It is not always as detailed as one might like but it may give you an idea as to whether your knowledge was lacking, your interview skills are weak, or there just weren't enough places to make you an offer. My advice though is to simply dust yourself down and remember that you have four other university applications to think about, so keep your fingers crossed for those.

Unsuccessful applicants almost never do anything wrong.
Admissions Tutor, Oxford

Once you have received all your offers or rejections from your selected universities or if you have received enough offers you have to inform UCAS of your firm and insurance decision. This means making a choice of where you would like to go, if you get the grades, and your second choice if you don't. If you are in the unfortunate position of missing the grades for your insurance place you can still apply to university through clearing in August. For more information go to www.ucas.com. Oxford and Cambridge do not have places in the clearing system though, so you will not be able to make a last-ditch attempt to get in that way!

Making the grade

In August when the A level exams come out, there are always mixed feelings. If you got the grades necessary to fulfil your offer then that's it – you're in and well done to you. If you did not, all is not lost.

First, you should get in touch with the Admissions Tutor as soon as possible. If you narrowly missed a grade they may let you in anyway. Call them to ask about this. Remember though, results day is a hectic day for all schools and universities, so if you simply cannot get through on the phone, leave messages and send an email and a fax too. You may find that the teacher who wrote your reference may have better luck getting through, so do ask for their help if they are around. If something happened to you or within your family in the last few months building up to the A levels then you must let the Admissions Tutor know, perhaps with a letter from your Headteacher. This could be something like a very serious illness or a death in the family. If this does not work, then you should accept your insurance offer from your original UCAS application. Hopefully you chose to accept an offer from a university which you are happy to attend. If this is not the case, then you could try to get into a different university by clearing (see the UCAS website: www.ucas.com).

> *The colleges oversubscribe knowing that some candidates won't fulfil their offer. If you are a few marks off the admissions tutors will decide if they will still offer you a place, in a meeting that happens on results day in August.*
>
> **Admissions Tutor, Cambridge**

An alternative to the above is to improve your A level grades over the next academic year. How many you retake and how long you need to spend doing so will depend very much on your individual module scores. Tutorial colleges are experienced in teaching retake courses and will advise you on your best course of action. If you do not need to spend the entire academic year studying you ought to ensure that you make plans for the rest of your time to be used advantageously. Universities will want to see that you have done something constructive with your time, such as charity work, learning a language or other new skill.

If you decide to apply to Oxford or Cambridge again, it is a good idea to apply to a different college. If you are asked whether you applied before do not be afraid to say yes. You will not be at a disadvantage. However, this is not true of medicine – medics feel that if you are serious about studying medicine you will accept a place elsewhere and would take a dim view of you waiting a year just because you did not get into Oxbridge. Your application must show signs of personal and academic development; these can be shown by your wider reading, your retakes, travels, and new skills learnt.

All this being said though, there is a lot to be said for moving on and not obsessing about Oxford or Cambridge. We are fortunate in the UK to have many excellent universities with first-class teaching and reputations which are recognised worldwide. If you are a motivated and focused student, then you will excel at whatever university you go to, and if you love your subject, then I am sure your passion will continue wherever you are. One of the most compelling reasons to apply to Oxford or Cambridge is because you are excited at the prospect of being taught a subject which you love by people who are at the top of the field in that subject. Remember that you can still have this at another university. If your motivations are like those I've described, you will not be heartbroken but will still look forward avidly to being taught your subject by specialists in another top university. If you do get low, and it is understandable to feel this way for a short time, speak to your friends, family and teachers to discuss your feelings and get a sense of perspective. Most students feel a bit glum for a while and then look forward to attending their new university. A few students end up getting really depressed. If you feel that this is happening to you it may be worth seeking professional help – maybe from a counsellor or your general practitioner.

> *More than 5000 unsuccessful applicants get three As at A level so they are not in any way unsuccessful students.*
>
> **Admissions Tutor, Cambridge**

Appendix 1: Glossary

- **Admissions tutor** – The tutor especially assigned the role of selecting candidates.
- **Alumni** – People who once went to the college but who have now graduated.
- **Clearing** – When the A level exam results come out in August, students who do not make their offers or, alternatively, students who get much better grades than predicted, can enter a competition for places at universities that have spare places.
- **Collections** – Exams sat at the beginning of each term at Oxford in the colleges.
- **Deferred entry** – This means you would like to take a gap year (i.e. defer your entry for a year). You apply this year but will accept a place in two years' time.
- **Deselected** – From the list of candidates who have applied for the course, some candidates will not have made it to the interview; they are 'deselected' before the interview.
- **Exhibitions** – A scholarship you can win in recognition of outstanding work at Oxford.
- **Go up** – Traditionally, instead of simply saying 'go to university' for Oxford and Cambridge the verb used is to 'go up' to university.
- **Open application** – A way of applying to either Oxford or Cambridge without specifying a college.
- **Oxbridge** – The collective term for Oxford and Cambridge.
- **Permanent private halls** – These are like mini-colleges in Oxford, two of them (St Benet's Hall (men only) and Regent's Park College (men and women)) are for any students, but the remaining five are mainly for people who are training to be in the ministry.
- **Pool** – The pool is the place where applicants who are rejected by their first-choice college are held in abeyance until another college selects them for an interview. The other college may do this for a variety of reasons, such as if they have not got enough good applicants and want to find some better ones, or if they want to check that their weakest chosen student is better than another college's rejected student – a sort of moderation process.
- **Porter's lodge** – Your first port of call at an Oxford or Cambridge college. This is where post gets delivered and where, if you get lost, they will be able to direct you – a bit like reception.

- **Read** – instead of 'studying' a subject, the verb used is to 'read' a subject.
- **Sub fusc** – The black gown, black trousers/skirt and white shirts Oxford students must wear to take exams.
- **Summon** – Another way to say 'to be called' for interview.
- **Supervision** – A class held on a one-to-one basis or in a small group with your tutor (in Cambridge).
- **Tripos** – Word used to describe how Cambridge degree courses are divided into blocks of one or two years, called Part I and Part II.
- **Tutorial** – A class held on a one-to-one basis or in a small group with your tutor (in Oxford).

Appendix 2: Key dates

Check these pages regularly to see if you are on track.

The year before you are going to apply

September

- Write your 'dream Personal Statement' (see Chapter 3).
- Start log book of lectures and events you have attended and books you have read.
- Start current affairs diary.

October

- Design your revision timetable.

November

- Revise very hard for your A levels.

January

- Sit A level modules.

March

- Request undergraduate prospectus from both Oxford and Cambridge and also the alternative prospectus from the student unions of both universities.
- Book yourself on an open day.
- Research other universities to which you are considering applying (you need to choose four).

April

- Write first draft of Personal Statement.
- Go on an open day.

Easter

- Revise very hard for your A levels.

June

- Sit A level modules.

Summer

- Ask friends and family to read Personal Statement and make revisions.
- Undertake work experience or voluntary work.

The year in which you apply

September

- Ask your teacher to read your Personal Statement.
- Visit the UCAS website (www.ucas.com) and register (get a username and password).
- Fill in the UCAS form (UCAS applications may be submitted from 1 September).
- Register for the LNAT.
- Book a time to sit the LNAT.
- LNAT (for people who want to study law at Oxford) can be taken on a date to suit you from the beginning of September.
- Register for the BMAT exam if you are applying for medicine (at Oxford or Cambridge) or veterinary science (Cambridge only).

October

- Fill in the separate Cambridge Supplementary Application Questionnaire. This will be emailed to you and must be completed by 31 October.
- The deadline for UCAS receiving your application form, whether for Oxford or Cambridge, is 15 October.

Late October

- Revise very hard for your A levels.
- Receive acknowledgement letter from your chosen college.
- Sit the appropriate aptitude test for your subject if there is one.
- BMAT exam (the actual date varies from year to year but is at the end of October or beginning of November) if you are applying for medicine (at Oxford or Cambridge) or veterinary science (Cambridge only).
- HAT (for history applicants to Oxford).
- Physics and maths for physics aptitude test (for physics or physics and philosophy applicants to Oxford).
- ELAT (for applicants to English at Oxford).
- PPEAT (for applicants to PPE at Oxford).
- Maths Aptitude Test (for applicants for maths or computer science to Oxford)

November

- Early November – sit the exams listed above if they fall in early November and not late October.
- Deadline for sitting LNAT (for people who want to study law at Oxford) is at the beginning of November.
- Receive letter inviting you to interview from Oxford or Cambridge and explaining if and when to submit written work.
- Submit written work with special form – see faculty website for details. (Work should be sent directly to the college unless you have made an 'open application', in which case send directly to the faculty. The work should be marked by your school).

December

- If invited, attend interview (most interviews are held in the first three weeks of December) (see precise interview dates for your subject in the prospectus).
- You may have to sit some tests at interview.
- At Cambridge you may have to sit the TSA.
- Before 25 December – hear outcome of application from Oxford.

January

- Beginning of January – applicants who have been placed in the 'winter pool' are notified (Cambridge only). This may or may not entail going to Cambridge for another set of interviews.
- Middle of January – hear outcome of application from Cambridge
- Sit A level modules.

June

- Sit A level modules
- After A levels sit STEP paper (maths only) or AEAs.

August

- Mid-August: results day
- If you have made your grades your place will be confirmed by the university.
- If you have not made your grades, contact the admissions tutor for your college.
- If your college rejects you, follow the advice in Chapter 9.

Appendix 3: List of colleges and some special features

Tables 6–8 list the various colleges in Oxford and Cambridge and their important, and in some cases, unique features.

Table 6: Oxford Colleges

College	Age	Size	Location	Special features
Balliol	Old	Large	Central	Has a nursery
Brasenose	Old	Large	Central	Next to library
Christ Church	Old	Large	Central	Large/has its own meadow and cathedral Accommodation for all 3–4 years
Corpus Christi	Old	Small	Central	
Exeter	Old	Medium	Central	Near library
Harris Manchester	Old	Small	Central	Near science area Only mature students over 21
Hertford	Old	Large	Central	Near library
Jesus	Old	Medium	Central	Near library
Keble	Medium	Large	Opposite university parks	Near science area
Lady Margaret Hall	Medium	Large	Far from city centre	
Lincoln	Old	Medium	Central	Near library
Magdalen	Old	Large	Central	End of the high street Has its own deer park
Mansfield	Medium	Small	Quite central	Near science area
Merton	Old	Medium	Central	
New	Old	Large	Central	Near science area and library
Oriel	Old	Medium	Central	
Pembroke	Old	Large	Central	Opposite Christ Church
Queen's	Old	Medium	Central	

St Anne's	Medium	Large	Far from centre	Has a nursery Near university parks
St Catherine's	New	Large	Far from city centre	
St Edmund Hall	Old	Large	Central	Has a graveyard; interesting grounds
St Hilda's	Medium	Large	Far from city centre	Used to be all female but started to admit boys in October 2008
St Hugh's	Medium	Large	Far from city centre	
St John's	Old	Large	Central	Near library
St Peter's	New	Large	Central	Near the Oxford Union
Somerville	Medium	Large	Far from city centre	Has a nursery
Trinity	Old	Medium	Central	Near library
University	Old	Large	Central	Oldest college in Oxford
Wadham	Old	Large	Central	Near science area and library
Worcester	Old	Large	Near Oriental Business School, Saïd Business School and train station	

Table 7: Oxford permanent private halls (PPH; bold indicates that they take undergraduates who are not mature students)

Permanent Private Hall	Description
Blackfriars	Only offers theology and philosophy. Very small. Central Dominican order. Mature students
Campion Hall	Mainly a graduate college. Very small. Near Christ Church. Jesuit order. Male only
Regent's Park College	Wide range of subjects and trains ministers. Large (for a PPH). Near Library Baptist Foundation. Like a 'normal' small college. Undergraduate
St Benet's Hall	Classics, English, history and theology. Large (for a PPH). Near Little Clarendon Street. Benedictine order. Male only. Undergraduate
St Stephen's House	Only offers theology and philosophy, for people who want to be ordained. Medium sized (for a PPH). Far from city centre. Anglican Foundation. For mature students over 25
Wycliffe Hall	Only offers theology and philosophy, for people who want to be ordained. Large (for a PPH). Far from city centre. Anglican Foundation students with families welcome. Mature students

Table 8: Cambridge colleges

College	Age	Size	Location*	Special Features I
Christ's	Old	Large	In city centre	
Churchill	New	Largest college	Not in city centre	Operates a shared nursery
Clare	Old	Large	City centre	Riverside
Corpus Christi	Old	Very small	Central	
Downing	Medium	Large	Not central	Science area
Emmanuel	Old	Large	City centre	
Fitzwilliam	New	Large	Not in centre	Near science area
Girton	Medium	Large	2 miles away from centre	Operates a shared nursery
Gonville and Caius	Old	Large	Central	Caius is pronounced as 'Keys' Has a nursery
Homerton	New	Large	Not in centre	
Hughes Hall	Medium	Very small	Not in centre	Mostly graduate/ mature undergraduates
Jesus	Old	Large	Quite central	Very sporty
King's	Old	Large	Central	Great for music due to their chapel
Lucy Cavendish	New	Small	Not in centre	Was women's only, mature students only.
Magdalene	Old	Large	Central	Traditional riverside – own punts
Murray Edwards	New	Large	Not in city centre	All female
Newnham	Medium	Large	Quite central	All female Very close to library
Pembroke	Old	Large	City centre	
Peterhouse	Oldest	Medium	Quite central	Accommodation for all 3–4 years Near science area
Queen's	Old	Large	City centre	On the riverside Has a nursery
Robinson	New	Large	Quite central	Close to library
St Catharine's	Old	Large	City centre	
St Edmund's	Medium	Small	Quite central	Primarily a graduate college but takes mature undergraduates over 21
St John's	Old	Large	Central	Accommodation for all 3–4 years Great sporting facilities. Riverside

Selwyn	Medium	Large	Quite central	Near Languages Near library
Sidney Sussex	Old	Large	City centre	Strong facilities for music
Trinity College	Old	Large	Largest college in centre	Very rich – good facilities and bursaries Riverside
Trinity Hall	Old	Large	Central	Accommodation for all 3 years
Wolfson	New	Small	Central	Graduate college, but admits mature undergraduates over 21

* Key: Quite central = 10 mins walk to centre

Oxford map

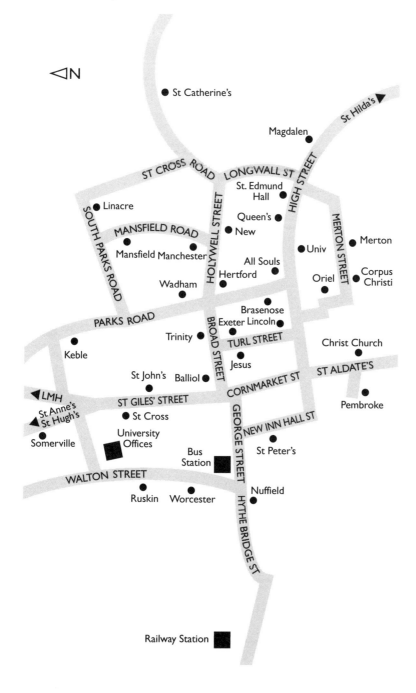

Cambridge map

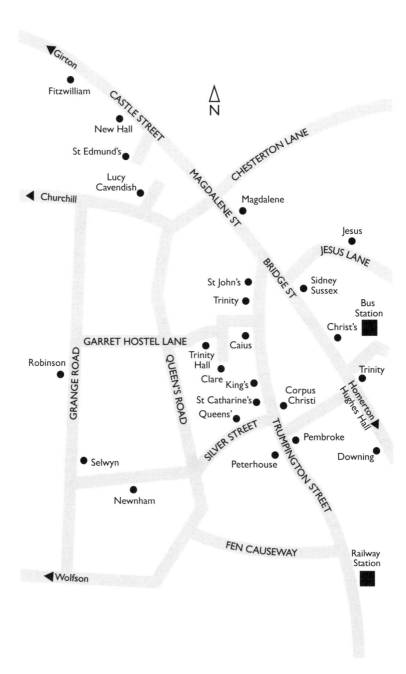

Postscript

If you have followed the advice in this book then you will have certainly given Oxford or Cambridge your best shot. Good luck and remember that you will be successful at whichever university you attend.

MPW (London)
90–92 Queen's Gate
London
SW7 5AB
Tel: 020 7835 1355
Fax: 020 7259 2705
Email: enquiries@mpw.co.uk